NO MORE PAIN

God Bless You!

Valencia D. Richardson

NO MORE PAIN

A WOMAN'S JOURNEY

FROM PAIN TO FORGIVENESS.

VALENCIA D. RICHARDSON

Y-NOT PUBLISHING
Mitchellville, MD 20721
www.y-notpublishing.com

Y-Not Publishing Company, LLC
12138 Central Avenue
Suite 197
Mitchellville, MD 20721

Edited by Laura Jackson
Copy Edited by Linda Nivens
Design by Deborah Leaner
Printed in the United States of America.

Visit Y-Not Publishing's website at
www.y-notpublishing.com

EDICATION

I would like to dedicate "No More Pain" to those who have helped to shape my life, to be who I am today. Because I have become strong, confident, successful, and now I can love others because, I have learned to love me.

Those who have helped shape my life are: My mother & my father, my grandparents, my husband, my children and my family. To all of you, I dedicate my book to you. I love you one and all, for loving me, even when I didn't love myself. You all have looked beyond my faults, and saw my needs.

My grandmother was amazing to me, and she was there to help me through the obstacles in my life, from the beginning of my life, until the last day of hers. Grandmother, I will always love you, and will always remember you as my "Ram in the Bush".

I will love you all for the rest of my life, because you have loved me. Thank you for loving me.

Valencia

II

TABLE OF CONTENTS

IV

$\mathscr{I}$NTRODUCTION

When I look at people today, I realize that like me, they have probably been through some heart ache and pain in their life. Whether in childhood, or adulthood, people experience pain, that may be hurtful to them for the rest of their lives.

You never know what someone has been through unless they tell you. The chances of that happening may be rare, but sometimes you will get the few who do share, and if they do, you realize that you are not alone in experiencing long term pain. Hopefully, this book will help you reflect on your pain, and you will decide that you don't want to hurt anymore, and you will decide to seek help either through professional means, or most importantly by seeking God, to help you through your pain. Maybe by reading this book, you will be able to start moving through your pain by applying some principals that helped me.

I wrote this book, "No More Pain" because I wanted to first of all, write down all of the pain that had gripped me for so many years and as I began to write, I realized how deep the pain in me was. There were times while writing, that I began to realize how much pain I was still in. As I wrote, my tears were cleansing, as the Lord began to wash away my anger, pain, my bitterness, and my unforgiveness. I was so tired of being hurt, and I decided I didn't want to feel it anymore!

The book is written in story form and hopefully you will be able to see some of yourself in some of my situations. If not, like my grandmother use to say, "Just keep on living".

Actually, this book is for those adults who have had a rough childhood that are trying to move forward from. As well as those adults hurting in their adult life from a recent hurt they want to get over.

Pain affects all of us at some time in our lives. Some have no trouble moving on, but for those who are like me, who suffered a lifetime from the pain caused in my childhood, this book is for you. Maybe you know someone who could benefit from this book, please let them know about, "No More Pain". Writing this book was cathartic for me because, I was finally able to get my pain out in the open, write it down, and share it with others, to get them to begin their healing process, so their lives can be changed, and they can walk in God's healing too.

I'm not all the way there yet, but I can attest to being a whole lot farther along than I was before writing the book and with God's love, guidance, and healing, and I know, if He can help me, He will help you too, just give it to Him and watch Him work a miracle in your life. I pray you will enjoy reading, be blessed and be enriched, by reading my book. God Bless You!

Love to you all,

Valencia

CHAPTER 1

FROM BIRTH TO SEVEN YEARS OLD

Valencia Richardson

If it weren't for the love of my Heavenly Father, I would not be here spending time with you or you with me. But because my Heavenly Father loved me so much and so well, I am here today. I count it an honor to be able to tell you my story. I hope that you can identify with some things I might say. I cannot say my life was very bad, nor has it been all good. But it is my life. After all I've been through, I can say I'm not ashamed because it has made me who I am today. I've learned to accept and be comfortable with the fact that I am me, the child my Father created. I'm not quite done yet. The one thing I know is I am my Father's child, He created me, He loves me, and nothing will ever change that. "For I am persuaded that neither death nor life, nor angels nor principalities nor powers, nor things present nor things to come, nor height nor depth, nor any other created thing, shall be able to separate us from the love of God which is in Christ

Jesus our Lord" (Romans 8:38-39).

I was born in a Washington, D.C. hospital during the winter of 1952. My parents were only married for ten months before I was born. They lived in my grandparents' home in a small suburb of Maryland called Jefferson Heights. There were only about 52 homes in the neighborhood. Everyone knew each other in this small town, as well as everyone's business. For the most part, they were good neighbors in that little community. As I look back, the best thing about that neighborhood was a small store across the street from our house. Growing up I was one of the store's best customers. I just loved the penny candy they sold and bought some every chance I could. Well, let me not get ahead of myself. My parents were only eighteen years old at the time of my birth. My mother had just completed high school and was unemployed while my father was a drummer in a band. As you could well imagine money was tight, so my parents moved in with my aunt and uncle who was my mother's oldest sister. The only income coming in was my dad. He would come home late at night after his gig, and sometimes he didn't.

Before I was born, my parents liked to party. Every time my dad would go out to play in his band my mother would want to go with him. She'd plead for him to take her, but he always refused. My mother loved my father so much. When she wanted his attention, she was dramatic. At times, she would run behind him, falling to the ground begging and crying for him to wait for her. However, he would only tell her to go back home, either with his mouth or by shoving her. This behavior went on even while she was pregnant with me.

One particular time after being gone for several days my dad came home late at night. He entered the bedroom and went over to where I was sleeping. While he was gazing down on my sleeping face, my mother decided she had had enough of his going off without a word and not even calling to check on me and how things were at home. In her anger, she decided this was a good night to put him out of the house. I can't blame her because if I were in her shoes, I would have done the very same thing. They separated when I was three months old.

After my parents had separated they briefly got back together. Shortly after, my father would move his young family to Philadelphia, Pennsylvania (his hometown). But before the move to Pennsylvania, my father continued to be gone for days at a time. During that time my parents lived with my grandparents in Maryland, they would feed them and buy milk for me.

My mother and biological father's wedding. My mother's oldest brother last on the right (leg got broken over the stolen bacon) The little boy is my oldest boy cousin I played with.

When my dad moved us to Pennsylvania, his pattern did not change. Daddy would be gone for days at a time; Thus, my mother would breastfeed me and go without food for herself. Somehow my grandparents knew we weren't eating right. One time they drove from Maryland to Pennsylvania to bring my mother groceries. After seeing my mother and the conditions we were living in, they moved us back to Maryland. Needless to say, my grandparents were angry about our situation. They told my mother, "If he's not going to take care of you and the baby then you might as well come on back home." We moved back to Maryland, which is where I subsequently grew up.

My first memory was at about one and one-half years old. It was traumatic for me, which is probably why I remember it so well. When my mother took me to the babysitter on her way to work, I was coughing very badly. The babysitter said very harshly to my mother, "You can't leave that baby here." She's sick! Hearing the babysitter say those words made my mother very sad. I didn't know it then, but times were hard in the early '50s financially and my mother had to go to work. It was traumatic for me because the lady was yelling, and very harsh in her tone. I remember my mom being very sad after what the woman said.

My next memory was sitting on the grass in a dressy white dress with my dog and being photographed by someone at my grandparents' house. I would learn later that it was my mother and stepfather's wedding day. I was the flower girl two years old.

My next memory was of me standing on my grandparents' sofa, in my pajamas, watching the soap opera, "As the World Turns," with my grandmother and great aunt (my grandmother's sister-in-law). I remember noticing that my grandmother and my great aunt were on the phone watching the story and gossiping about the story line. I noticed because my grandmother was very expressive and intense, and emphatic about what she had just seen or heard in a scene. I also remember that my grandmother and great aunt kept calling each other after every commercial to talk more about the scene they had just watched. This behavior between my grandmother and great aunt would continue daily. I liked to see my grandmother get excited and express herself with great vigor.

It soon became apparent to me that I was living with my grandparents. Though I knew my mother because she would often visit, it became obvious that I was staying overnight and during the day with my grandparents. At that time, I did not know anything was different about me living with my grandparents. It was life as usual for me.

I remember my male cousin lived in the house behind us (his mother was my mother's oldest sister). He was three years older than me. We played every day because my grandmother babysat both of us. He taught me to throw rocks, eat dirt, eat berries that grew on the berry tree in the back yard. Introduced me to the store across the street from my grandparents' house that sold candy. He also taught me how to get money often to go to the store by sneaking money out of our grandmother's purse. Our grandmother had several purses that always had change in the bottom of them. So without me knowing what I was doing, my cousin taught me how to steal money from my grandmother. Later after we had grown up, I told my grandmother what we did as kids. She threatened to give us a whipping even though we were adults, but she never did. I so loved my grandmother! Even though I had a mother that I often saw, I still always felt that my grandma was my mother, too.

For several years, I lived with my grandparents and would stay with my mother and stepfather on a lot of weekends. Though I was never told why, it was fine with me. I was happy and never felt the need to inquire.

Grandparents

While living with my grandparents, I realized my grandfather was the one who spoke at our church every Sunday. I soon came to know that not only did he speak at our church every Sunday, but he was the Pastor of our church. I didn't know what that meant then, but somehow I realized he was in charge of our church and must be a very important person. He often met with other people who came to our house in a room my grandparents called "the study."

My grandfather pastored a small church in Seat Pleasant, Maryland. When he became the pastor there were only two members. He would preach each Sunday to those two members, and because he was a good preacher, the church began to grow. When he retired twenty-nine years later, there were 1,500 members. The church was small, but it was a close-knit group. It seemed that most people knew and loved one another.

When we were at church, people always wanted to shake our hands and talk to us. I learned later on that people always like to be around the pastor's family because it made them feel important. All I knew was people always would rush to our different family members after church to talk or shake hands. It seemed that everyone wanted to be our friend. I didn't want to be their friend because as a kid, I didn't know them, and they were grownups. All I wanted to do after church was go home, eat dinner and play with my cousin.

As I got older, I began to think that we must be pretty special people because everyone wanted to be our friend; I found out later people just want to be associated with those in power. It wasn't about us at all. When my grandfather retired from the pastorate and became the No. 2 person as pastor emeritus, the same people that used to want to be our friends suddenly befriended the new No. 1 man; the new Pastor. I'll talk more about that later.

I remember those early years as being years of love, great discoveries, and uncertainties. I will always remember the joy I felt when my grandmother would make me and my cousin homemade ice cream and warm chocolate iced cupcakes. We would sit in the yard on hot summer days. After my cousin and I would play hard, our reward at any given time would be our grandmother calling us to come and partake of those delicious treats. Man, those were the good 'ole days for me!

I remember my aunt (my grandparents youngest daughter) lived with us, too. She was okay, but she never liked for my cousin and me, to be around her much. Oftentimes my grandmother would make her watch us when she had to go somewhere with my grandfather. My aunt resented that job, as any teenager would. Often she would make us her slaves when my grandparents left the house. While she talked on the phone, she would make us run errands for her – get her water, soda, food, or whatever – while she would lay there on her assets on the sofa. If we did anything to make her mad, such as not doing what she wanted us to, she would be waiting for our grandparents to come home so she could tell on us. Most of the time we did not get in trouble except to be told to behave ourselves next time or else.

One time when my aunt was babysitting me, she had a friend over to the house. My grandparents had left to go to a church meeting, and I set the bathroom on fire. I had seen my grandfather smoke a cigar from time to time. I was about five years old when I decided I wanted to have a cigar. So I went into the bathroom with cigar and matches in hand. I stood in front of the mirror so I could watch myself smoking this cigar. After several attempts, I lit a cigar and finally took my first puff. As I began to choke and coughed my head off, I heard my grandparents walk in the door. They asked my aunt where I was. In a panic I broke the cigar in half, and threw both half's in the trash can that was full of paper. Meanwhile, I ran out to greet my grandparents and tried to keep them from going into the bathroom right away.

My grandparents immediately smelled smoke. Suddenly the trash can caught on fire and smoke filled the room. My grandparents called my aunt and me. I became horrified as I stared at the fire blazing in the trash can before me. They asked my aunt if she had been smoking. She assured them she had not, and they realized it must be me. I was back in the bathroom trying to figure out how to extinguish the flames when they rushed in and saw me standing there. They pushed me out of the way, put the trash can in the bathtub, and turned on the water. In horror, I saw the flame go out and immediately wondered why God had not been kind enough to show me that trick before my grandparents did. The feeling of "Lord, I'm coming home" came to mind at that moment, as I awaited my impending execution.

Though I did live to see the next day, my feelings were very hurt as was my backside. For the first time in my life, I had made my grandparents mad at me, and that hurt me so much! They weren't too pleasant for a while. My mother made a special trip to her parents' home just to visit me. For the first time, I realized she was not very happy to see me either. I knew she loved me when my grandparents asked her not to spank me, because that had already been taken care of by my grandfather. She gave me a stern warning about what would happen to me if I ever did that again. Since the Lord had spared my life, I vowed to Him never to smoke cigars again. That was the day that the God my grandfather spoke about every Sunday became real in my life. For several weeks after that incident, I'm sure I sang His praises from experience. Oh, what He had done for me, Hallelujah!

My cousin who lived behind our house was always getting into trouble because he was hard-headed. He stretched the limits as far as he could, and that did not set too well with my grandparents. As I recall, he got a whipping every day for something he had done wrong. That never seemed to matter to him much – the whippings I mean – because the next day he was back breaking the rules once again. He was older than me and seemed to know things I did not know.

Once when I was six years old, my cousin asked me to go into the shed because there was some cool stuff in there. I went in with him. After he had shown me things I did not find cool at all, he asked me to pull down my pants and let him stick something in my butt. "Why?" I asked. He said, "Because it will be fun, you will see." After saying no about twenty times, I was tired of being asked and said okay. Well, all I knew was he was trying to put something soft and mushy into my butt, but it would not go in my butt. Boy was I glad because the reason I was saying no was because I just knew it was going to hurt. I did not know that something was wrong with it.

My uncle (my mother's oldest brother) walked in during my cousin's attempt to put that mushy thing in me and asked what were we doing? My cousin said, "She asked me to put something in her butt." I said, "No, he said he was going to put something in my butt." My uncle told me to go in the house, and he talked to my cousin. Well, the next thing I knew my uncle came in the house with my crying cousin. He told my grandmother that he found us in the shed doing something. I did not know what he said we did, but I was shocked that everyone was so angry.

I was so hurt when my grandmother sharply said to me, "I am trying to raise you right, and you are out here doing all the dirt you can do!" I didn't have a clue what she was talking about when she said that. What dirt? I knew what we were doing in that shed was not good. My grandmother gave me a spanking and said not to do that again. Then she made me take a nap.

A few hours later, my mother came to my grandmother's house. She told me she was going to whip me. Not because I knew what I was doing was wrong, but because she had told me never to pull my pants down in front of a boy, no less my cousin. It finally dawned on me I was wrong because I had disobeyed my mom. At the end of my whipping from my mom she screamed, "Now I am going to send your father in here to whip you, too!" "Oh God," I cried in my spirit. Today is the worst day of my life. "Another whipping? I cannot take another one. Please God, have mercy on me. I am just a kid!" You will see later on how saying I'm just a kid can come back to haunt you someday.

Well, God heard my humble, terrifying cry and pitied every one of my groans. Praise Jesus! When my father came in, he asked, "Do you know what you did was wrong?" I replied yes. He said to my surprise, "Well, I think you have had enough whippings for one day, so I'm not going to whip you. But don't do that again." I swore with all my strength that I could muster up never to do it again. When my father left the room, I felt so, so blessed. I cried, "thank You, thank You God!"

Even Now when I think back on my early years, the time spent with my grandparents and playing with my cousin still comes to the top of my list as some of the best days of my life. Just imagine partaking of fresh, warm, homemade yellow cupcakes with chocolate icing. I can smell them now — just coming out of the oven and homemade ice cream.   Yum!

Those were the good 'ole days. Just writing this makes me feel happy, peaceful, and content.

With good, there were also bad moments. I remember I had a friend that lived next door. She had older brothers and sisters. One day I went over to her house to see if she could come out to play. Her older brother told me to come in the house. He pointed and said, "she's back there." So I went back with him. Suddenly he said, "Do you want this?" I looked, and he had his erect penis out. I was so scared. "No," I said. He said, "Don't you want this?" I screamed no and ran out of the house. I told my aunt who lived with us and told her not to tell my grandparents. She said okay but told them anyway. The next thing I know my grandfather was going over to the house next door. I did not know what he would say or do. My only fear, since I was no longer in danger, was that my friend would never speak to me again for telling on her brother. I was never allowed to go into my friend's house again. Though she kept asking me why I couldn't go into her house, I never told her what happened that day. I just said I don't know why my grandparents would not let me. I was embarrassed to tell her what her brother did to me.

I awoke one morning to find my grandmother packing boxes. "What are you doing?" I asked her. She said we were moving. "Why are we moving?" was my next question My grandmother said, "You're grandfather, and I are moving." "What for?" I asked. "And who is going to take care of us?" meaning me and my aunt. My grandmother said, "Your aunt is my daughter, she has to go with us." Where am I going to live?" I asked as a feeling of abandonment began to grip my heart. I think my grandmother thought her answer would make me happy, which is why she did not tell me the whole story right away. I think she wanted to surprise me. When she told me the answer, my heart sunk. "You will stay here and live with your mother and stepfather. They are moving in when we move out," she said. Well, I thought to myself, it may be all right for you to move without me, but it's not okay with me. I felt abandoned. I didn't know my mother. "I don't want to live with her all the time," my grandmother said. "But she's your mom." I went into the other room and cried because I was so hurt my grandmother would leave me with strangers. It was not a happy day for me, not at all. Did anyone know what I was feeling? Does anyone know that I'm hurting right now? My grandparents are leaving me in a place that always felt like home because they were there, and love was there.

"How can they leave me" I asked myself? Although I was only seven then, and I will never forget the loneliness and pain I felt on that day. No one but God knows what I was feeling that day, no one but God! I could not share my feelings with anyone in my family because I did not want to hurt anyone's feelings, and I didn't want anyone to know I felt unloved and abandoned. Even though my heart was breaking, I tried very hard to hide my tears.

The last year I lived with my grandparents was in 1959 --I was seven years old. I would continue to spend time with my grandparents some weekends and on Sundays during church. Often we would have Sunday dinners at my grandparents' house with all my aunts, uncles, and their families. My grandparents had six children – four daughters and two sons. When I saw the movie Soul Food, it reminded me of those days long ago at my grandparents' home. I would learn then and as time went on that spending time with family is the best thing ever.

I loved my grandparents so much! My grandfather was a serious man, but he was also very funny. He loved my grandmother and his children. He loved me and his other grandchildren, too. He was dedicated to his church and church family. Sometimes he would get up in the middle of the night to go and counsel one or more of his parishioners. I could always go to him with a question about God or His Scriptures, and he would answer the question in a way that a child could understand. I would discover that his children would also ask him questions about God and Scriptures. It seemed we all (his family) depended on him for spiritual knowledge, guidance, and understanding.

My grandmother was like my mother. I knew her as my caregiver who cared for and loved me very much. I loved her and felt very close to her. I went to her for wisdom and compassion. I cried with her and told her what made me happy and sad. She was always there to comfort me throughout my whole life. Because of her love for me, I will always appreciate what she did for me. She always made me feel a part of her immediate family, always accepted me, and always showed me love. She cared for me when I was sick and was always gentle. She taught me how to love other people. She taught me right from wrong. Before I knew Jesus, she was my rock. And after I met Jesus, she let me know that she could still be my rock because He was her rock. That was powerful to me.

$\mathscr{C}$HAPTER 2

MAMA DRAMA

My mother age 15

A major incident occurred just after my parents moved in my grandparents' house. I heard a large commotion as I played in the front yard. The noise came from the back. I ran to see what was going on, but my grandmother would not let me into the house. She told me to stay away from the door and go into the yard. I did, but the terror I felt would not go away. Suddenly, my grandfather, stepfather, and grandmother came running out of the house with my mother in their arms. They put my mother in my stepdad's car. My stepfather went to the driver's seat as I cried. I asked my mother where she was going. She replied she was going to the hospital. I could only scream, "Why?" But she was silent. At that moment, I noticed the white gauze wrapped around both of my mother's wrists. What happened to her? The car sped off. I asked my grandmother, crying and in a panic, what happened and would my mother return? My grandmother just replied, "Your mother hurt her wrists" and she assured me she would be back. My grandmother told me during another conversation that my mother used to have spells. She said she would stare off into space sometimes. I did not find out until I went to college that the spells my grandmother spoke of were focal seizures. She said my mother did not have them anymore, so I never talked about it again. Let me say, I never asked nor was ever told why I lived with my grandparents. I was just happy and comfortable there. I knew who my mother was. I just thought our mother-daughter relationship was different from other mothers and daughters. The only difference was I lived most of the time with my grandparents. The thought didn't concern me at the time. However, it was a question that would be answered much later when I was an adult.

In 1959, my grandparents moved out of our small home in Jefferson Heights into a large home in northeast Washington, D.C.. My grandmother's aunt and uncle, Mary, and Issac Scott owned the home my grandparents moved into. Mary and Issac worked for President Woodrow Wilson. They were personal assistants for the President and First Lady. Often you will find in early documentary clips of President Wilson riding in a horse and buggy that my uncle drove. There are also pictures of my uncle standing on the steps of the White House waiting for the President to come out for public appearances. Later, after President Wilson's term ended, my aunt and uncle would join them at their new home on S Street on Embassy Row in Northwest D.C., where they cared for them until their deaths. Embassy Row is where the embassies of other countries around the world are headquartered. The Wilson's loved my aunt and uncle, and Mrs. Wilson gave my aunt some memorabilia from each of them. Before she died, Mrs. Wilson also gave my aunt and uncle her third addition memoir. I remember a few times as I went through school that my grandfather would bring all the memorabilia to my history and civic classes to show the children and teachers. I vividly remember sitting in my history class in 11th grade. As we watched a history documentary film, I saw my uncle riding President Wilson in a horse and buggy from the White House to another destination. Surprised because I did not know such a film existed, I yelled out "that is my uncle!" The students asked where? When I pointed him out to them, they said, "No, it's not." The next day my grandfather proved to them that it was him. My teacher and classmates were so impressed when my grandfather brought the goods to class and gave a history lesson regarding my aunt and uncle.

Well, let me get back to my thought. When I lived with my grandparents in Maryland, I would go to my parents on the weekends. I never felt comfortable there because I did not know my mother. Yes, she was nice to me. I had my own bedroom with a brand new bunk bed, but I just never felt at home. Have you ever been in a room with people you did not know? While you're with them by yourself, you fish for things to say to each other. But all along you wanted to go somewhere that you felt more comfortable? Maybe wish someone would walk into the room that you knew, so you would not have to endure the pain of the experience alone? That is how I felt being with my mother. I would pray for Sunday to come so I could go back to my grandparents' house.

I remember thinking, "I should want to be with my mother." After all, my cousins liked being with their mother.

What child would not want to be with their mother? I did not understand what was wrong with me.

My mother and stepfather moved into what used to be my grandparents home with my uncle (he was the youngest). His wife and their two-year-old daughter moved in, too. I was very happy that I wasn't going to be living with my parents alone. The very idea of being around just my parents was dreadful. I enjoyed having someone to play with after the sun went down. My uncle always made us laugh, and my aunt liked me. So I learned to accept my circumstances. Them being there was a bonus for me.

After settling into our home as a family, I learned quickly that my parents loved to throw parties. I can remember lying in my bedroom, located above our basement and listening to the sounds of Dinah Washington, Billy Holiday, Etta James, Ray Charles, and others. As the parties went on into the night, the partiers would begin to sing to the records. All the records! I thought it was so funny because some of those voices were awful! But the longer the party continued, the more they sang. During this time in my life, I realized my love for music. It is also where I discovered why they sang so horrible the longer the party went on. My parent's parties exposed me to drinking and cigarettes. That certainly did not go on when my grandparents lived there. It was then that I decided maybe living with my mother would not be so bad. After all, I was learning about some new things.

I wanted to stay awake for the entire party, but I would eventually drift off to sleep. When I was able to stay awake, or awakened by a loud noise, I could hear people talking with slurred speech, and I was trying to figure out who it was talking. I was surprised that the people I knew would sound funny after being at my parents' parties. They did not sound like the people I knew. Before the saying, "What's up with that" became popular, I was wondering back then, what is up with these people's voices? Often, arguing, cursing, loud, angry voices, and laughing voices would awaken me. When the parties ended, the noise would go upstairs to my parent's bedroom. I did not know what was going on in there at the time, but it was very happy in there. I am sure my grandparents had happy times in their bedroom, but I never heard anything like what I heard coming from my parents' bedroom. There were times I heard very loud arguing coming from my parents' bedroom, too. As I began to hear the happy sounds on a regular basis though, it seemed to make me happy as well. It made me wiggle. And I discovered that touching certain parts of my body when I heard those sounds from their bedroom made me feel very good inside. I did not know then that I was experiencing the joys of sexuality and masturbating at the early age of seven years old. A counselor told me that because I was feeling so good and sexual during those times from my parents' bedroom, I must have had someone sexually assault me at an earlier age. Other than what my cousin did to me in my grandparents shed and the neighbor exposing himself to me. I cannot think of any other thing that would cause a child to feel sexual from hearing lovemaking sounds coming from their parents' bedroom. Neither of those episodes mentioned earlier conjured up any sexual feelings within me. Unless I discover otherwise, I will stick to my thoughts that a child can experience sexual feelings from hearing lovemaking sounds. I discovered that by touching myself when I heard those sounds, it caused me to feel as good as my parents must have felt. Somehow I was relating what I heard with what I felt when I touched my private parts. There were times when I knew I had an orgasm, at the same time my parents did. That, as I look back on those times, I think those experiences were amazing! That is how I feel about my experience. That is my story, (and unless someone can give a better explanation for what I felt at my age and why), I am sticking with it.

My mother was a very passionate woman, and she loved people. If she loved you, you knew it. And if she did not love you, well, you knew that, too. She loved to have a good time, and she was not afraid to express herself. If you got her wrong (as she would say), you were going to hear exactly how she felt about it "in no uncertain terms!" It never bothered her that not only could I hear her making love, but so could her brother and sister-in-law. To her all of it was natural, and she was not going to hide her feelings from anyone. Once I was an adult, I told her that I heard her and my stepfather making love. She had no problem with it at all.

Everyone knew these things about her. So when she got drunk and acted out by cursing, yelling, and fighting, everyone was mostly quiet, or they would try to calm her down. No matter how crazy she got they would not yell or curse back at her because that would just make her madder. If she fought them though they would usually try to protect themselves. They understood, but I didn't. I would be so sad and embarrassed when she would drink and act out. I did not understand why she always had to get mad and start fights. There were times when some new person would join the party, and if they were drinking, my mother would start getting angry with them. If a person had any sense, they would just shrug off her drunken anger and taunting. If they did not have sense, they would soon find out that encouraging a fight was not a smart thing to do.

I recall when a co-worker of my mother came to our house after work, and brought a friend with her. My mother had never met the friend. They started drinking, and the friend kept talking harsh, loud, and cursing. She said negative things about my mother and my mother's co-worker. When my mother had enough of the woman, she grabbed her by her collar and dragged her to her co-worker's car. She put the friend into the back of the car, and she got in the passenger's side. The co-worker got in the driver's seat. They drove to the friend's house. My mother got out of the car, dragged the friend to her front door, and said, "Do not ever come to my house again," and left. We never saw that woman again.

That was my mother. I love her and always will! No matter what you hear in this book about my mother, she was my mother. Certainly she wasn't perfect, but she was my mother nevertheless. You only get one mother in this life, and I have learned that no matter who they are, they will always be your mother. God gave you the mother you have for better or for worse, and for a very good reason. I promise you this one thing … I will never forget my mother nor will you forget yours.

CHAPTER 3

SCHOOL YEARS TO COLLEGE

I began school at age five while I was still living with my grandparents in Maryland. Tommy, my two friends (Charlene and Tanya who lived across the street), and I would all walk to school together. We walked about a mile each day. One day Tommy told us he had found a short cut to school. We really wanted to know that shortcut because school seemed like such a long way to have to walk. He didn't tell us where we were going, but just said to follow him.

The next thing we discovered was we were walking through a graveyard. My friends and I were shocked. Leave it to Tommy to find the scariest place for a five and two six-year-olds to walk, especially when he told us dead people were under those big stones. Well, Charlene and Tanya said we could walk to school through a graveyard if we wanted to, but they weren't going to. I was afraid to walk to school by myself, so if they didn't go to school I had to walk through the graveyard with Tommy. Tommy would always try to scare me. He would say, "Mr. so and so is chasing us, you had better run!" I would run as fast as I could; even though I didn't know whom Mr. so and so was. My cousin loved to scare girls, so he enjoyed scaring me all the time. One day my Aunt Tina took us to a park called Glen Echo, which was the only park in our area with rides in the early '60s. Tommy convinced me to ride the roller coaster. I had never been on a roller coaster, so I didn't know what to expect. I was so gullible then. Once the ride began, we started going up a large incline. On the way up, I thought we have to come down from this high hill.

When we got to the top and I looked down, I just knew I was going to die. I started to scream as the car began to go down. Devilish Tommy started to pretend he was pushing me out of the car as he laughed hysterically. I started to cry when I discovered we were going up the hill again. I kept screaming I want to get off, let me off! The more I screamed and cried, the more Tommy pretended to push me out. He pushed me back as we went up and pushed forward as we went down. He laughed and laughed. When the ride was finally over and we were approaching, the ride operator who was a little older than my cousin saw my tears, the terror on my face, and my disheveled appearance. What did he do? He sent the ride up again. I was terrified that I was again going to go through the torture I had just experienced.

I was so mad, still crying and screaming stop this thing! We only went back up one time and then the operator stopped the ride. "Don't do it again," I screamed to the operator! I quickly got off the ride, and ran and told Aunt Tina what Tommy had done. She said she would tell grandmother when we got home and Tommy would get into trouble. That was satisfying for me to know. I could not wait to see what would happen to him when my grandmother found out. It was worth the wait. But to this day I have never ridden another roller coaster. I developed a phobia to roller coasters because of that traumatic incident.

I was in the second grade when my parents and I settled into my grandparents' home. School was okay, but I preferred to play more than anything else. I could not wait to get home so my friends and I could play. The best time was playing on the weekends because we could play outside all day long.

I remember just before second grade, my first teacher when I was in kindergarten. She appeared to be very, very old to me, but she was also nice and I liked her. I would see her many years later while taking care of her at one of the hospitals where I worked. I knew her right away, but she had a mental disorder and did not know me. I felt so obligated to take good care of her and treat her as my special patient, and so I did just that. I so wanted her to see how far I had come because she was the first teacher who taught me, but that was not possible with her condition. I remember thinking that I hope when she gets to heaven someday, she will remember that I took care of her just the way she took care of me all those years ago.

I remember one day watching the Pic Temple Show with my cousin and seeing two children who had given a carnival in their yard for Muscular Dystrophy (MS). The kids had raised $100 and were presenting the monies to Pick Temple for children suffering from MS. Theresa and I thought that was a great idea and we could be on the show too! I talked to my mother about having the carnival in our backyard and to my surprise, she said yes. I was so excited! On the day of the carnival, we had pin the tail on the donkey, bobbing for apples, darts and lots of candy. Everyone had to pay to play the games and we had prizes for the winners. That was a fun day and we raised $50.00. Theresa and I dressed alike for our interview with Pick Temple on his show. In those days, there was no taping of shows, so everyone saw us on the show, except Theresa and I. The joy of being there was worth so much more to us.

Another time we raised money for another cause and

went on "The Miss Connie's Show." What I remember most about that show was unusual. I remember meeting Miss Connie just before the show and being shocked to see her smile with very yellow teeth. Unfortunately, that was the only thing I remember about that T.V. appearance. First impressions can make a very powerful and lasting image on the mind of anyone, but especially on a child.

When I was twelve, the drinking and fighting had become so frequent that I was really getting worried about my mother and depression filled my spirit. Once after one of my parents drinking parties, my mother got drunk and fell. She hurt her leg and it bled quite a bit. As I laid in my bed that night, I began to cry and the tears would not stop rolling down my face. I decided to call the doctor the next morning. I called the military hospital where we would go to get treatment for illness. I was connected to a counselor. I asked the counselor if he could help my mother who could not stop drinking. He asked me how old I was, and I told him I was twelve years old. He said the only way your mother can get help is if she asked for it herself. I said, well that is not going to happen. He said, "I'm sorry little girl that is the only way we can help your mother." I became even more depressed and sad because I knew my mother well enough by then to know she would never go to a doctor because she did not think she had a problem with drinking. I also knew that I was not the one to ask her to get help because I had also learned by then that my mother would get mad at the drop of a hat and you never knew what would light the spark. Sometimes the thing you thought would not make her mad would make her mad. There were also times when my mother was very depressed herself and the next day, she would be so happy. You would wonder what happened to make her so silly and happy. Her happiness was extreme at times, as well as her depression being extreme at other times. I noticed that when she had one drink, she was calm. Three drinks would make her mushy. She would always want to kiss and hug me. Five drinks would begin to make her irritable, and after about eight or more drinks, she would become very drunk and very mean. I never knew what kind of person would wake up in the morning, a happy mother or a mean mother. I hated her mood swings and I felt like I was always walking on eggshells until I found out which mother I would greet each morning.

I got quite a few whippings during my school years. Even when I didn't know what I had done; I might get threatened with a whipping from my mother. If she were in one of her mean moods, she would think of a reason to whip me for the littlest thing. Once she asked me when was the last time I had a whipping I said, "I didn't do anything,", but before the day was done I would get a whipping for something. That happened several times throughout my school years. Oftentimes I was not sure my mother loved me because she could become real mean to me. The times when she was nice and happy though seemed to make up for those hard time.

My stepfather, Earl was in the Air Force. When I was thirteen years old, after returning home from him being stationed in Fort Worth, Texas, my cousin who lived behind my grandparents' home, before they moved, introduced me to a boy at church. He said they were best friends. The boy was almost three years older than me. He was cute and I liked him. I did not know that this boy would be a significant person in my life. We fell in love and began to talk on the phone.

My mother said I was too young to date, so we were phone and church friends. We began to go steady and before long, my mother said we were getting too serious, so I had to break up with him. At fourteen, my grades began to fall. That's only because I realized I was really beginning to hate school, and yes, I would rather talk to my boyfriend rather than to study. Well, each time grades came out each quarter, I would get a whipping and punished. I could not watch T.V. or go out to play. The punishment lasted two to three weeks and I would have to break up with him, my mother said. I was on punishment so much I was too embarrassed to keep breaking up with him. I felt like he must have thought I was such a baby and a dumb one at that. I always told him the breakup was because of my grades.

Once, my boyfriend and I were to go to a dance at my school. It was my sixth-grade dance and as I stated my boyfriend was almost three years older than me. I never asked my mother how we would get to the dance but since my boyfriend had a car, I assumed we would go in his car. I was too afraid to verify that with my mother so, on the day of the dance, I spoke with my boyfriend and he stated he had washed and waxed his car so we could go to the dance. We were both very excited about the dance. When my boyfriend pulled up to the house, I was ready to go, when my mother pulled her coat out of the closet. I had a puzzled look on my face and my mother said, "You didn't think you were going to the dance in his car did you"? I said, I thought I was and she said, I told you that you are not old enough to date. My boyfriend and I were very disappointed I could see the surprise on his face when my mother said, "I'll be driving you to the dance. Again, I felt like a baby. I wanted to know how he could like someone like me who had so many restrictions, but thank God, he did.

My mother was still drinking heavily during this time, and I was getting to the point where it got on my nerves. I was always embarrassed whenever we would go anywhere, and she would get drunk. No one else's parents got as drunk as my mother did and she would always get a "drunk look" on her face that I hated very much! It was a look of being too drunk to be in control, eyes closing and opening very slowly and lips twisting with slurred speech. The look would make me very angry, but I had to keep it to myself as I watched her have that look over and over again.

My mother was a mean drunk and very strict on me. I could not always trust her love for me, and the fact that I had to walk on eggshells, was really causing me to continue in my depression. I guess that is what most teenagers think about their parents that they are too strict, but in my case it was true!

My time in sixth grade stands out in my mind for two reasons. The cousin that lived with us with her parents (my mother's baby brother and his wife), was in kindergarten when I was in sixth grade. My classroom faced the street in front of our school. That is where my grandfather would pick my cousin up every day after her half day in kindergarten. The problem with him picking her up was often a meeting he had would run over and he would be late picking up my cousin. I would sit in class, turned around looking to see if my cousin was still waiting for our grandfather, when suddenly an eraser would hit me upside my head. When my teacher was lecturing the class is when I would turn around. I can understand that I was not paying attention, but I was worried about my little cousin. She was only five and she would always cry when things did not go the way they were supposed to. I told my grandfather that I kept getting hit in the head with an eraser when he is late picking my cousin up. I also tried to explain to my teacher why I was not paying attention. He understood, but he said he still wanted me to pay attention. The situation improved a little with my grandfather picking my cousin up on time more often. However, when he didn't I would still occasionally get hit in the head, but my teacher had a little more mercy on me.

The second thing I remember about the sixth grade was one day as my teacher was lecturing the class, someone came into the classroom and whispered something in his ear. My teacher appeared visibly shaken. I wondered what was wrong, as I am sure my classmates did as well. The same person left the room and brought back a T.V. with him. A T.V. I thought, oh boy! Well that oh boy was short lived when the T.V. came on and there was Walter Cronkite telling the world that President John F. Kennedy had been shot and killed. What a shock! My teacher had tears in his eyes and so did many of us. We did not personally know the President, but we all loved him. He had made a lasting impression on America and his family was becoming very well known for their political legacy. While I knew that Abraham Lincoln had also been shot and killed, I never thought that would ever happen again because it occurred so long ago. Who would kill our beloved President? All of the people in the United States and abroad mourned the loss of such a great man. That was the first-time death had touched my heart so deeply and I prayed it would never happen again for as long as I lived.

I remember when I was ten years old, my mother came into the bedroom where I was and presented me with two birth certificates. It seemed that by handing me the certificates without saying anything that she thought I would understand what they were. One certificate had a different last name. The other one had my last name that was familiar to me. I asked my mother what they were. She told me that my stepfather was not my real father. My real father's name was on the first certificate. What a shock! I never knew that my stepfather was not my real father. I knew he was not affectionate to me or my mother. In fact, that was always an issue of contention between them. My mind was suddenly flooded with a whirlwind of questions. Since he is not my father, is that why he is not affectionate to me? Where is my real father and why did he leave me? I was angry that my mother and stepfather deceived me. I wanted to know why the rest of my family did not tell me all of this. I was so confused and just wanted to be alone with my thoughts. I cried and cried and did not trust anyone for a while. I really felt that this was not fair. One thought was, why out of all my cousins, was I the only one with a fake father? I felt like an outcast in my own family.

Eventually, I was able to accept the truth, but I did not like it at all. I was adopted by my stepfather. It would be a long time before I would appreciate what he had done for me. I asked my mother if I could meet my real father, but she said she did not know where he was.

During these years of school, my mother, stepfather and

I would move from our grandparents to a small community in a city called Glover Cove, Maryland. We lived right around the corner from my aunt and uncle we lived with in my grandparents' house. We moved into a new housing development. We were only in that house for two years when my stepfather was ordered to serve in the Vietnam war. My mother and I stayed in the new home until he returned. He was gone less than a year. When he got back from overseas, my stepfather was ordered to serve in Atwater, California. I was almost eleven years old. I remember while in California once, my parents were having an argument. They were physically fighting and I stepped in to stop it. During the scuffle, I was injured and discovered my leg was bleeding. That ended the fight. My mother called the military police and my stepfather was arrested and sent to jail. That arrest would have caused my stepfather to be in a lot of trouble with the military, so my mother did not press charges.

We were in California for fifteen months when my stepfather was ordered to serve in Fort Worth, Texas. My father went to Fort Worth early, while we stayed behind to sell the house. Once the house was sold my mother and I drove to Fort Worth, Texas.

In order to get to Texas, my mother had to read a map. I guess she was very anxious about the drive and she put the weight on me. She told me since I was taught to read a map in school, I should be able to help us get to Texas. "What?" I said to myself. I do not know how to get to Texas. They never taught me how to get to Texas in school. My mother was really depending on me to get us there, so at night I would study the map and chart out our course for the next day. I was terrified that I would get us lost and if I did, my mother would be mean and disappointed in me. Since she was counting on me, that was a very stressful time. I felt that my mother should try to read the map herself, but I would not dare say that. I was scared of my mother, and since I was not always secure in her love for me, I always tried to please her. This meant I would not get into trouble or make her mad.

We were only there for three months when one night at a party, my mother found out my stepfather was having an affair. Well, the next thing I know, we were in the car driving back to Maryland.

My mother would not let me express my feelings to her if it were something she did not want to hear. If I questioned her too much and she was in a bad mood, or did not want to be challenged at that time, she would scream, "Just shut up." That is when I began to write poetry because I had to express myself somehow. So I started to become a deep thinker. I would think about my circumstances, my mother, my biological father, my stepfather. I would ask myself, "Where is the love?" There seemed to be no consistency of love in my immediate family. I would go to my grandparents' house to be loved and pampered. I would ask my grandparents what was wrong with my mother, and my grandmother would always say, "Honey, your mother's got some problems. All we can do is pray for her." Meanwhile, I thought I have to live with her terrorism.

I would never tell anyone other than my grandmother how much I was hurting, or how mean my mother was to me. I would always pretend that everything was okay with the rest of my family. As a matter-of-fact, I became a comedian in my family's eyes in order to cover up the pain. I cried so much during my school years.

My mother would embarrass me in front of people whenever she felt like it. Once I got a pair of gloves for Christmas from one of my mother's friends. She came to see us and brought gloves. When I opened the gloves, I said, "I have a pair just like these." I was not disappointed in having two pair; I merely made a statement. Well my mother yelled at me in front of that lady, and said, "When someone gives you something, I don't care if you have 100 pairs like them, you be grateful because they didn't have to give you anything! Now go to your room!" Gee! I thought to myself, I didn't know that was a bad thing to say. There were many situations like that that came up when I was growing up. I learned many valuable lessons that way. The worst embarrassment I experienced was when my mother would get drunk around others. Especially my friends because I felt like my mother was the only mother that was drunk. The men would get drunk all the time, but my mother was the only mother to get drunk. It seemed I was always walking on eggshells; I never knew what to expect at my house or out of my house. It was an uncomfortable feeling and believe me, the stress level of living like that is unbelievable!

I often wondered why my mother drank so much. I discovered that alcoholism was very prominent in our family. My grandmother told me that some of her brothers and one of her sisters were alcoholics, and my grandfather had alcoholism in his family.

The second reason I feel that my mother drank is because being a pastor's child is not easy. People are always looking at the first family of the church to be perfect. I was taught that we always had to watch what we did or said because it may be a bad reflection on the pastor.

Three of my grandparents' children were very rebellious. They drank heavily and would hide their negative behavior from everyone except their family and very close friends. They would also try to hide their behavior from my grandparents. They all became alcoholics.

The third reason I think my mother drank so much is possibly from a condition that I spoke about earlier with her spells. I will speak more about that later.

My mother and stepfather stayed together in the house because we could not sell it before going to Texas, so my mother rented it out. When my father returned from Texas after we did, they decided it was cheaper for us to stay in the house until it sold. When the house sold, my mother and I moved into a Maryland apartment near the Washington, D.C. line. My mother and stepfather divorced. I felt very protective of my mother. We had never been on our own. We were in the apartment for one year. My mother decided she needed to save some money so she moved in with her baby sister and her husband. She said I could stay there too, but space was very limited. A deacon and psychiatrist from our church asked me how the living arrangements were for my mother and me. I told him they were okay, but it was not a lot of room for all of us. He asked my mother if I could stay with his family until my mother got back on her feet. She said, "Yes." I agreed because I was friends with their daughter.

After my mother and I had gone to our respective places,

I settled in with the deacon's family. He told my mother that he would help me through the divorce. Even though I felt abandoned again, it was good having someone to talk to, who seemed compassionate and understanding of what I was going through. I did not like having to be separated from my mother, but I knew she needed to save some money in order for us to get a nicer apartment of our own. While I tolerated the separation, I did wonder why it was beginning to seem like I was always being abandoned. In addition, feelings of rejection were becoming clear within my heart. I began to wonder why I had to live with my grandmother when I was little. Why my father left me when I was a baby? Why my stepfather left us? Why did my mother keep making me leave my boyfriend, whenever my grades were not to her liking? I was beginning to feel that I was not good enough for anybody to hang around.

That prayer that I would never go through the pain of loss again lasted just a few years. In the twelfth grade, many of the guys had enlisted in the military to fight in the Vietnam war after graduation. The next thing we knew Robert Kennedy (President John Kennedy's brother) and Rev. Dr. Martin Luther King Jr. were shot and killed.

Growing up during the civil rights movement, and Dr. King was an African American's hero and for many Caucasian's as well. He marched for equality of all men and woman. He went to jail for his and our God-given right to be free from oppression, discrimination, and hatred. He was a sojourner for truth and righteousness, and a drum major for peace and non-violence among all people. His death was a tremendous loss for his family, friends, his wife, four little children, and for our nation. Who would stand up for our freedom now? Many tried. Rev. Ralph Abernathy, Rev. Jessie Jackson, and many others, but there was no one to fill his shoes. My thoughts were why do good men and woman die when they are doing so much to help humanity, and make clear to the world our inalienable rights that "All Men Are Created Equal." We the people have made some strides in our rights since Dr. King died, but slowly in this time period of our lives, it appears that there are those who would love to take us back to where we were so many years ago. It is wrong, unfair and will not be acceptable if we the people have anything to do about it.

During my school years, my mother dated a few men and they all drank. But none to the extent that she did. Eventually, my mother would remarry. My stepfather also remarried. This time my mother married a man who owned of all things, a liquor store. I thought when I found out, "oh no, this is not going to be good." The good news was the guy was nice. He liked me, loved my mother and most importantly, I would not be living with them to see the drama that owning a liquor store would bring. This would be my mother's third and final husband. There was as much drama with him as with the others because the drinking got worse. The accessibility to the alcohol was too tempting for any alcoholic and there was drama in their marriage. After graduating from high school in 1970, I was ready to decide what to do with my life. College came to mind. My mother had always told me that education was important. I had struggled with school because I did not like doing the hard work. My mother never let me get away with that excuse and was very hard on me when my grades were not A or B quality. Since she instilled in me, I should go to college, I decided to do some research. I decided since I was always a counselor to whoever asked for my advice, I would become a social worker. Well, when I found out I would have to go to school for six more years, I quickly changed my mind on that career. I told my mother I would go to college four years instead. To my surprise after all the education hype, all of the stress on me about my grades, she did not have the money to send me to college. I finally decided what I would do with the next four years of my life and now, there is no money to do it. What a disappointment. I told my mother I would get a job. She said she never wanted me to work and go to school (probably because she understood my struggle with school), but what else can I do? I thought you had no money to send me to school. I immediately became depressed about my situation and I was angry with my mother and stepfather for not saving money for my college. I was devastated!

While watching T.V. one morning, a commercial came on the T.V. that claimed, "You can be a nurse!" Freedman's School of Nursing at Howard University in Washington, DC was looking for those interested in helping others to apply. There was a catch. IT WAS FREE! Not only was it free, but they would give you a monthly stipend for your expenses.

Now won't God work it out for you? That was nothing short of a miracle! I called my mother at work and told her the good news. She could not believe it. It was such a miracle that she had to call Howard University herself to find out if that was true. She was so grateful and so was I. It was settled, I would be a Registered Nurse. Not only that, but I could stay on campus at Howard University and get away from my crazy, chaotic home and mother!

Joseph and I had broken up so many times by the time he went off to serve in the Air Force at age eighteen. We communicated a little, but then he went his way and I went mine two years prior to my high school graduation.

I remember when I was sixteen and in the hospital recuperating from surgery for a ruptured ovarian cyst and appendicitis, I got a letter from Joseph. He wrote, "I heard you were in the hospital for surgery, I hope you are feeling better." I was so happy to hear from him—until I got to the last paragraph. It simply said, "I'm getting married in May and we'll be stationed in Turkey." I was crushed! How could he do that to me? We loved each other and said we would get married. I know my mother kept breaking us up, but that did not mean he could marry someone else. As I lay in my hospital bed, tears rolled down my face. I thought and said to myself, I cannot ask him not to get married because he already proposed to the girl. I thought I would not want anyone to do that to me. I was not ready to get married though, but I did not want him to marry someone else. There is nothing I can do about it. It's too late. I have been abandoned and rejected once again. I was hurt to my very core. My mother did not seem concerned about his impending nuptials but said she wished him all the best. The fire and hatred I felt at that moment for my mother burned a whole in my tongue. If only I could say to her what I wanted to say at that moment. If I could, I would have yelled to the top of my lungs, "it's your fault, all of this is your fault. You made me break up with him so many times, to get what you wanted and now he has gotten fed up with it and has left me for good and it's your fault. I hate you so much!"

I went into a real funk for several weeks after receiving my boyfriend's letter. My mother did not think that we were serious about each other to get married, or she did not want us to get serious because she did not want me to get pregnant. She once told me when I told her I loved him, "You don't know what love is, that's just puppy love." I wanted to tell her, you don't know what love is either, but I would not be alive today if I had dared to utter those words to my mother.

My feelings about my mother at that point in my life was I loved her when she was not drinking. But when she was drinking, I hated to even be around her. I would leave the room where she was and go to my room, in hopes that she would leave me there alone. Depending on how bad things got on any given episode of her drinking, I hated her and wished her dead, especially if she was embarrassing me. I learned the meaning of "It's a thin line between love and hate."

By the time I was sixteen, I had taken more risks with telling my mother how I felt. When I could not take the risk, I would write either a letter or poem about my feelings. If my mother thought I went too far in expressing my feelings, she would tell me to shut up, or she would often say, "I hope when you have children, you'll be the perfect parent!" Or she would say, "You must think I'm a monster." I thought being a perfect parent will be a piece of cake. That is until I had children of my own.

To this day, when my children tell me about my problems, I remember what my mother said. I always said I would never be like my mother. I will not drink, smoke cigarettes or anything she did. My mother gave me quite a few whippings until I was fifteen years old. As I look back, some whippings I did deserve, but there were many that I got that I did not deserve. Even as an adult, I still feel that way.

My ex-boyfriend came back to Maryland when I was nineteen years old. He was still married but wanted to date me. I told him that I did not date married men.

Soon after his return, he separated from his wife and eventually got a divorce, after being in Turkey for four years. He and his wife had her third child and his first, a son, while in Turkey. She had two children by other boyfriends before they married.

We both realized we were still in love and absence had made our hearts grow fonder of one another. He told me that even though he was married, he had carried my picture in his wallet the entire time he was in Turkey. We were married six months after I graduated from College.

As for college, I entered Howard University in 1970 at age seventeen. I went all out that first year. I partied hard, began smoking cigarettes, started drinking, had sex for the first time at age eighteen, and just had a great time. I was sheltered from everything outside my home and I wanted to explore what else was out there. I had a sense that I never had freedom in my home because my mother was so strict, now I wanted to do my own thing and that is exactly what I did.

Nursing school was hard, and partying did not help. After the second semester, I had to go to summer school or run the risk of flunking out. When I realized that my chance to become a nurse was in jeopardy, I immediately woke up.

I did not want to be a failure in anyone's eyes and especially my own. I simply could not handle that thought! During my college years, I must admit my mother was there for me. Every day I wanted to quit. The work was so hard! Our instructors were very challenging, especially when we did what we called our clinicals, (that is when we had to work with actual patients in the hospital, guided by the instructors). That was when the real pressure came. You got your assignment the day before. The assignment consisted of the patient's name, diagnosis, and other medical problems and what you needed to do as a nurse to help that patient, while also following doctor's orders. We then had to go to our room and study what we would do to help the patient based on their diagnosis and other medical issues. We had to write down what we would do for the patient, based on the information we had gathered the night before. You had to consider everything about this patient's condition and method of treatment and what you would do for them, and how you would teach the patient what to do for him or herself to improve their condition.

If you had missed something in your study the night before, your professor asked you about it the next day. They would embarrass you in front of the patient, other students, or worse, make you immediately stop taking care of that patient because you did not know what you were doing. They would then step in while you watched them do what you could have been doing had you been prepared.

Being embarrassed was not one of my strong suits in the social arena. I hated being embarrassed because my mother did it so often. It would make me feel useless, dumb, and not good enough. I began to realize that they were trying to help me learn, and when they embarrassed me, I would study harder the next night for my assignment the next day. I know my mother was trying to help me, too, but sometimes my mother was just being mean and abusive. The longer I was in nursing school, the more I prayed. And the more prepared I became, the less embarrassed I was.

I graduated from nursing school, and I was proud of what I had accomplished along the way, with the Lord's help and my mother on my side. My grandmother would tell me she always prayed for me every day, so I thank my grandparents also. I think my mother prayed for me, too, but I am sure it wasn't as much as my grandmother did. My grandmother could pray, and whenever she prayed aloud, she always made me cry.

The fact that knowing my grandmother would pray for me every day meant she understood my plight. Despite what I had been through, she wanted me to succeed. I believed it when she told me that she prayed for me each day. I would thank the Lord that I had someone in my corner that was close to God, praying for me. She was praying for me and I knew that her prayers would make it through to God, and He would help me to always make it through.

She knew her daughter, and she knew she didn't always do the right thing by me. She felt helpless because my mother was volatile sometimes, and after all, she was just the grandmother. She knew that my mother had to raise me and she would pray that I would be able to make it through anything, unscathed.

My grandmother would tell me when I'd tell her some

of the things my mother would do or say to me, "God will always provide a ram in the bush." I found out what that really meant, as I look back over my life and see how far the Lord has brought me. I discovered that though my mother was not the best mother, my grandmother was there for me as the ram in the bush. God provided for me, in my mother's stead, when she could not be the mother that I needed.

The road through nursing school was tough, but the reward was sweet. My mom was so proud of me. I had to and did thank her for all of her encouragement during nursing school. Every day I called her to say I was going to quit, and every day she encouraged me to stay. She would say, "You can do the work." All the years she made me feel like a second-class citizen about my grades, she finally believed in me and wanted me to know that.

The feeling that I had for my mother on the day I graduated from nursing school did not heal the pain I had experienced with her, from the age of seven. But it helped me to know on that day that she really did love me and wanted the best for me.

After graduation, the beginning of my nursing career, my marriage, and having children would soon reveal all the fear, insecurities, and hurt that had built up in me since leaving my grandparents' home when I was seven years old.

$\mathcal{C}$HAPTER 4

MY LIFE: WIFE, MOTHER, NURSE, SALVATION!

I must admit I drank in college, but I had never smoked marijuana. But once my boyfriend and I started planning our wedding I began smoking marijuana and hash. I never had a desire to smoke it before. My fiancé smoked it while in the military stationed in Turkey. I felt comfortable with him, trusted him totally, and loved him very much. I wanted to be a part of whatever he did—so I started smoking. We were married on January 19, 1974.

For our honeymoon, we went to the best hotel in Washington, D.C. (at that time), which was the Stattler Hilton. We paid $100.00 a day, which was a lot of money in 1974. We brought with us two bottles of wine and an ounce of marijuana. We spent the next four days in the room making love and getting high. We thought we were living large and were very, very happy.

We returned from a wonderful honeymoon to learn that my husband's two-year-old son from his previous marriage would be living with us. He was a handsome little boy. We settled in our new marriage, a son, and our new careers. My husband found a job working in finance after getting out of the military.

Life was more difficult than I thought it would be; mainly because I didn't plan on a child so early in our marriage. I didn't know that would cause me to harbor negative feelings against my husband, for hurting me when I was sixteen by suddenly informing me that he was getting married. I would soon begin to resent his son and started taking it out on my husband. We began to argue a lot, and I did not know that I had not forgiven him for getting married. We were always supposed to be married, and he had the audacity to hurt me with the greatest hurt a woman could feel – betrayal.

We argued so much my husband eventually developed an ulcer. At first the doctors couldn't figure out what was wrong with him. Finally, they diagnosed him with an ulcer. The night we got his diagnosis I left the hospital and went home. I stood in the mirror and cried out, "Lord what do you want me to do?" Then in a clear voice I heard the Lord say, "Forgive him." Right then, I realized that all the arguments we were having had been because I had not forgiven him. Wow, what a revelation! I told the Lord at that moment that I would forgive my husband. He had been so sick, and I was afraid I would lose him. Thank God, He gave me another chance to make it right with my husband.

A few months later, my husband's ex-wife wanted her son to come back home to her. We took him back to his mother in Virginia, which is where he grew up, when my mother found out; she came over to our house one night, drunk as a skunk. Before she knew the whole story, she said that my husband was going to leave me, and I should be ashamed of myself for sending the baby back to his mother. What she didn't know was that we were not sending him back because we wanted to; his mother wanted him back.

The next day, my mother and I met at a restaurant on our lunch hours. I tried to explain to my mother why we were sending the child back. I was very upset that she would come to my house drunk late at night and accuse me of sending my husband's son back without knowing the whole story. I cried the entire time, and my mother was embarrassed that I was crying in front of all those people in the restaurant. I had a right to cry after what she did to me last night in front of my husband. I was furious with my mother, and I did not care who saw me crying. My mother was trying to stop me from crying so she would not be ashamed. At that moment, I did not care about her feelings because last night she hadn't cared about mine. How could my mother plant a negative seed inside my husband's head towards his wife? Would he leave me? I felt betrayed by my mother.

After my husband recovered from his ulcer, and my stepson went back to live with his mother, we began our life as husband and wife. It's funny how God healed this situation. But I still had doubts and was seeking more. I had been saved since a small child, yet I don't believe I knew what I was doing until the day one of my cousins gave me a song.

In May of 1976, I was about five months pregnant with my first child. Life appeared normal until my cousin contacted me with a song. It was in my voice range, and she wanted me to practice it. The message in this song was so incredible to me. It had to be fate that she would give this to me to draw me into the Lord. I would soon realize just how much I loved and needed Him. The song was by Danni belle Hall entitled, "Great Is thou Faithfulness." I remember how this song resonated with my soul. I listened to it several times the night my cousin gave it to me. On my way to work the next day, I listened to it over and over again. While at lunch, I listened again and even had a co-worker listen to it. This song became my theme song for the day. The song continued to draw me, and when I rushed into the house, I sat on my hamper and asked the Lord what He wanted me to do. The next words that came out of my mouth were, "Lord, just come into my life."

I immediately called my cousin and screamed, "I just asked the Lord to come into my life!" She praised God with me and stated that the Lord had told her to give me that tape. "Well, it worked," I said. I was so full of the Holy Spirit I couldn't wait to tell my husband. When he came home from work that evening, I was so fired up in my spirit; talking non-stop about the time God and I spent together. I went on to tell my husband that I asked God to come into my life. The amazing thing about that day is that after my husband had heard my testimony he said, "I want that, too." I led my first person to Christ that very day. I would later read in the Bible that "With the heart man believes unto righteousness, and with the mouth confession is made unto salvation." I had believed in Christ and immediately told my cousin how her fulfilling prophesy played out in my life. I had reached out (to my husband) and preached the gospel, and he believed. That was a tremendous day! Our marriage was blessed so much more that day and in a few months we would receive another gift from God.

In October of 1976, my husband and I welcomed our first child —a beautiful baby boy. I loved him so much I couldn't wait to bring him home. We enjoyed being parents and watching our baby boy grow. We gave him my husband's first name, and my grandfather's middle name. One thing I will never forget about this little boy was that he loved his mommy's homemade sweet potato pie. I asked him if he wanted cake or pie for his second birthday and to my amazement he said pie. I gave him his birthday pie. His little sister was just as peculiar as her brother.

Our second child — a beautiful baby girl — was born when our son was twenty-two months old. My mother gave her the first name, and I picked the middle name. She was so beautiful, but I felt she was going to be a handful because I was in labor for sixteen hours. The day I brought her home; I laid her on the bed to change her out from the hospital clothes, but she screamed and screamed as if I was taking too long. By the time I gave her a bottle, she was too mad to drink it. It took a while to calm her down. Her poor brother felt so sorry for her because she kept crying and crying. Eventually, she settled down. These memories I cherished because I was able to stay home with each child and learn who they were. With our son, I stayed for three months but after our daughter was born, I stayed home with both of them for a year and a half. That time was so special for us. I am so glad I was able to do that.

Our daughter and her brother loved each other. I remember how she would boss her brother around. Once when she was around three years old I heard him tell her, "You are not the boss of me, only mommy and daddy." She is still bossy to this day! She has a son now who bosses her around, and she gets sort of upset about that and will complain to me that he bosses her around. All I can do is laugh and reminisce. As they grew older my husband, and I knew we needed to introduce them to their older brother. At the age of fourteen, my stepson came back to live with us. Even though it was a short time that he stayed, the three of them were able to make some connections. He and my daughter were very close. I just wish he and my son were able to bond just as easily. After spending quality time caring for my children, I had to return to the workforce. I was an RN, but I wanted to be an operating room (OR) nurse every since childhood.

As a child, I recall a movie scene where the doctor and nurse were in the operating room, and the scrub nurse was slapping the instruments into the surgeon's hand. You could hear the slap. At that moment, I said that is what I want to do. An opportunity arose at a hospital in D.C., and they were training nurses to become OR nurses. That movie I had seen so long ago came to mind. I decided to apply for a position there. I was on my way to reaching a dream that I had as a child. The nurse in the movie seemed to have control and command over those instruments. Before the doctor could even say what instrument he needed, she slapped it into his hand. It was amazing to watch, and I wanted that control and command. I eventually became a scrub nurse just like I saw in that movie so long ago. Surgeons often praised me because I, too, could anticipate which instrument they needed before they asked for it. That made me proud. Only God could help someone be able to achieve that, and all the glory belongs to Him.

I believe that God has allowed me to see happiness in my adult life, and for that I am truly grateful. I do not want you to think that my issues with my mother ceased to exist even after God had brought me so far. My mother's drinking was still an issue that now didn't affect just me but my children as well. There was a time I told her that if she didn't stop drinking I would never let her care for her grandchildren. The one time

I agreed to let her keep my children was a disaster. When she returned my children to me, she was drunk. Her boyfriend was with her, so he drove, thank God! I couldn't believe she got drunk while my kids were in her care. I was furious with her. How could she do that after I told her what would happen if she drank while she was keeping them? I told her that was it! I would never trust her to keep my children again. She told me, "You'll be sorry." I responded, "No, you'll be sorry."

My mother was sorry after that. Every time she knew my husband, and I went out, she would ask, "Who is keeping the children?" She would immediately get jealous when I told her my mother-in-law was keeping them. I knew it hurt her, and it hurt me, too. My kids were missing valuable time with her that she would never get back. What else could I do though? I would take them to see her sometimes, but by this time, I was so frustrated with my mother's continual drinking without even attempting to stop. Another time I asked her to go see a psychiatrist with me so he could help our relationship. She stated that I was the one with the problem, not her. When I was growing up, I felt that she chose the bottle over me, and I believed that about her relationship with my kids as well. I felt that I was not worth much to her if she could not stop drinking, knowing how much I hated it. Just the way it seemed she chose men over me, she chose the bottle over me. That is a hurtful, hurtful feeling when you are talking about your mother. Most of the time, I was not sure whether she even loved me because of the way she treated and talked to me. It seems crazy to feel that your mother doesn't care for you sometimes, or love you all the time, and expects you to love her. My mother saw things differently no matter what she had done or said to you, she expected you to give her the utmost respect; this is how I felt most of my life. I sometimes felt that I was a visitor in my mother's life because she wouldn't be bothered with me. That is not a healthy, wholesome, or acceptable feeling for a child to have their entire life. Those feelings don't just go away once you become an adult. They often linger, sometimes for a lifetime.

$\mathscr{C}$HAPTER 5

MY ADULTHOOD REVEALS MUCH

My graduation from nursing school; I'm on the left side, 3rd from the top next to the railing.

Once I became an adult, I began to hear stories about my mother when she was a child and the issues she faced throughout her life.

My mother told me about a time my grandparents gathered their six children to sit down for breakfast. Just before eating, they prayed for their food. When they finished praying and opened their eyes, my mother discovered her bacon missing. While everyone's eyes were closed, someone stole my mother's bacon from her plate. She immediately blamed her oldest brother. He denied taking it, and before you knew it; my mother had wrestled her brother to the floor and when the smoke cleared her brother's leg was broken.

The funny thing about the whole incident is her brother didn't take the bacon … My grandmother had. My grandma would always give to her children and husband first. She must have been real hungry to take my mother's bacon. That was the way my mother would react to some situations in her life, everyone knew it, and they laughed to keep from crying I guess. I think most people were a little afraid of my mother because of the way she acted at times. I know I was! I tried to please her and do whatever she told me to do because I did not want to encounter her wrath. Often when I did get in trouble, she would say, "You better never do that again, or I will half kill you." I used to think; half kill me, I know that will hurt if I am half-dead and have to feel all that pain. Just kill me I thought, and be done with it.

My grandmother told me that one time she and my grandfather were sitting on their front porch in D.C., and heard an ambulance drive by on another street. My grandmother said to my grandfather, "I think that is our daughter" (my mother). Sure enough, in an hour, they were called to the hospital because my mom had a mental episode and had to be hospitalized. I never found out what happened, and my grandmother did not like to talk about what my mother's issues were. She was trying to protect her.

Another time, I found out that my mother went to visit her pregnant youngest sister. At some point during the visit, my mother suddenly pushed her down a flight of stairs. My aunt lost the baby. That story made me sad. My mom and her baby sister always had trouble communicating, but I didn't know what happened this time to cause her wrath. They would eventually work out their problems, but things were different between them for a while. That period made me very unhappy because we were a very close-knit family. When we experienced conflict, it hurt all of us. I didn't like conflict, but it was very present in my life.

Sometimes when my mother got mad it made me angry! I would as respectfully as I could tell her that she hurt my feelings. My mother would then tell me a story about how my grandfather's cousin wanted to adopt me when I was two years old. She would then tell me how she had thought about it because they had so much more to offer. When it came time to give the cousin an answer, she had said no. She wanted to keep me.

Whenever I would hear that story, I never knew if my mother was trying to send me on a guilt trip to prove how much she loved me, and I should not criticize her. Then maybe she was trying to tell me that I should be forever grateful to her for not giving me away. Whatever her reason, I felt it was mentally abusive. Often I felt that way given the way she treated me, maybe I would have been better off had she given me away. However, when things were good between us, I was glad she didn't.

I stated earlier that my mother married three times. After her divorce from Paul, he would treat me as if I was no longer important to him after meeting his second wife who had four children. After my mother and Paul divorced he treated me differently. All of his attention was on his new wife and her four children. That was a painful period for me. He couldn't see that his new wife was creating a barrier between him and me. His new wife pushed him to focus on her and his new family. At first I didn't care because I was still angry at him. Because of his affair our family was destroyed. But when he started bringing his new wife around friends he and my mother shared, I felt that was very disrespectful.

By the time I was preparing to get married, my mother had married her third husband — the owner of a liquor store. He seemed to love my mother and our family. He even offered to pay for my wedding. My other stepfather did not offer any help, so I did not ask him to give me away. He had a new family and did not seem to be too concerned about me anymore. My stepfather Paul didn't seem to care what was happening regarding the wedding and never offered any financial assistance. Since he wasn't concerned about my wedding, or me I didn't ask him to give me away. He had a new wife and family; I was part of the past. My new stepfather gave me away since he contributed to our wedding, which helped to make it a success. A few months after the wedding Paul's wife called me to say I had hurt him by not asking him to give me away. This woman had done everything in her power to keep my stepfather Paul out of my life once they married. Now she was calling me to talk about hurt feelings? I wanted to say why didn't Paul call me for himself? You don't have anything to do with this so shut-up! But I didn't. Instead, I told her that her husband didn't offer to pay for anything for the wedding, so the honor went to the person who had, my stepfather George. She couldn't say a word after that. I'm sure she played a major part in my stepfather (Paul) not offering because he had to take care of his new family. Eventually, I apologized to my stepfather (Paul) for hurting his feelings. But I also told him the same things I told his wife. I was bitter.

My mother and new stepfather were happy for a while, but her drinking escalated. George brought two teenagers to the marriage, a boy, and a girl. By this time, I was in college.

Due to my mother's escalated drinking, I stayed on campus most of the time.

I went home for the weekend once. As I opened the front door, I saw a very large terrarium my stepsister had given to my mother for Christmas broken into pieces at the bottom of the stairs. Someone had obviously thrown it down the stairs. My mother was in her bedroom, and my stepfather and stepsister were in the kitchen talking. I asked what happened to the terrarium. They both said your mother threw it down the stairs. I asked why she did that. They said she was mad at my stepsister. I told my stepsister that I was so sorry for what my mother had done. I know she paid a lot of money for that large, beautiful terrarium and even if she had not it was wrong of my mother to destroy it that way.

I went to my mother's room to find her looking sad and embarrassed. I asked her what happened, and she told me the same thing my stepfather and stepsister had said. I asked her if she had to throw the terrarium down the stairs? I told her that was not right. I decided to turn around and return to school because, I did not want to get in the middle of that mess and frankly, I was ashamed of my mother.

It was just five years after their marriage that they got a divorce, mostly due to my mother's drinking and meanness to my stepfather's children. My mother felt guilty about all the things she had put her husband and his children through during their marriage. My mother always felt guilty after her drinking episodes if something bad had happened. That was the status quo for her. She would not drink the day after a traumatic episode but would soon resume her usual pattern shortly after that.

As a child, beginning at age twelve, I have felt the need to look out for my mother and protect her. During her drinking years, she would fall and injure herself, get into fights, drive while under the influence, and have blackouts. I worried about my mother more after each of her divorces, because I felt that while she was married her husband would look after her unless she had an altercation with them. When she was not married, I always felt it was my job to take care of her. I worried when she would go out by herself because I knew she would get drunk and drive herself home. Normally, unless she told me before hand that she was spending the night somewhere, I would be up half the night worrying and waiting. That would soon prove to be very annoying and made me resent having to be my mother's keeper. I felt I was forced to become a parent. I wanted to be a child. I longed for someone to take care of me and care about me all the time, not just some of the time.

I mentioned earlier that I would try to please my mother to avoid conflict. Even when I knew she shouldn't leave a young teenager home by herself all night. Often she would ask me if I mind if she stayed out all night. I would say no because I knew that was what would make her happy. To be honest, I was terrified to stay home all night by myself. I wouldn't tell my mother that because I feared she would think that having me was holding her back from having fun. So I would pray a lot when she left me home by myself all night.

I think it was the Lord, who gave me the idea to sing while I was home by myself. On my fifteenth birthday, my mother and first stepfather gave me a stereo console with a microphone. I was terrified when I was home alone in the evening. Whenever I was, I would put on some records, plug in my microphone and sing my heart out just to make it through. I was so grateful to the Lord each day I woke up and realized I was still alive. God helped me make it through with my music. Why didn't I call anyone in my family? Because I did not want anyone to know that my mother was leaving me alone. As a matter of fact, I never talked about what was going on at my house with my family, except to ask my grandmother questions I was really concerned about. I would also talk to my aunt that had lived with us before the first divorce. She always made me feel better. I knew that what was going on with me and my mother was not right, and I did not want anyone to ever feel sorry for me. I tried always to keep a stiff upper lip in the presence of my family and others.

But at night, all bets were off. I put my head in my pillow and would cry me a river. That is when I realized my God was a comforter. After crying, I would always feel a sense of peace, at least for a while. I would feel like I could make it one more day. Those hard times with my mother were lonely times for me. I believe my depression began during my childhood, but I will talk more about that later.

I was amazed that my mother could be drunk as a skunk on Saturday, and go to church and sing in the choir on Sunday. That is what she did for years. Towards the end of her drinking, she would get drunk during the weekdays and still get up and go to work the next day. This was also the time when "three martini lunches" were acceptable for some workplaces. People would have those drinks and go back to work. I remember calling my mother one day after her lunch break. I could not believe she was drunk at work.

I did not know what to say. I said, "Ma, how could you be this drunk at work?" How could she keep her job? It's funny; people swore by their "good government jobs!" They would say, "If you've been working in the government for years and years, it was difficult for them to let you go." Well, I guess it was true because my mother did keep her job, or maybe God was extending her A LOT of grace.

I was proud of my mother's career. She began working as a nurse's aid. Then she moved into the social work field in the government and worked her way up with training and additional courses. Finally, she received a license as a social worker associate.

Once I got married, I realized how mentally exhausted I was from all those years with my mother. Though I would continue to worry about her, I was somewhat removed. Since I wasn't living in the home, I didn't know what she was doing.

I remember just before giving birth to my first child asking my mother what it was like carrying me and giving birth. This isn't an unusual question for a first-time mother to ask her mother. My mother said, "I don't remember." So I asked her what it was like when I was born and as the baby. Again, she said, "I don't remember."

I was shocked, saddened, and deeply hurt. I thought to myself, how could a mother not remember what it was like being pregnant or the early years of her child, her only child. Did she not think about me growing inside of her? Did she not savor every time she felt me moving within her? Every mother that I know longed for the day their baby would kick her for the very first time. I felt like I didn't matter to her. I felt unloved and so unimportant to my mother.

I wanted to shout out loud to my mother, do you know how much it hurts me right now that you don't remember my beginnings? It broke my heart once again. At that moment, I vowed to savor every moment of my children's lives.

I forced the very thought of my mother not remembering me inside of her or my early years into the recesses of my heart. That memory slowly drips blood from my heart, even today.

While my mother couldn't remember her pregnancy or my early years, she later said she remembered the labor pains. She said the labor was so bad she wanted to kill herself. She said that she asked the nurse to open the window (the hospital was not air-conditioned), but the nurse would not do it because, she knew my mother would jump to her death. What a hurtful thought that on the day of your birth all your mother remembers is that you caused her so much pain she wanted to kill herself. What hurt even more is that my mother would say these hurtful things with a straight face. It seems she was oblivious to the pain that she caused me. As a result of the verbal abuse by my mother throughout my life, I developed low self-esteem.

$\mathscr{C}$HAPTER 6

SORROW STRIKES AGAIN

Top Left, my mother, top middle, mother's baby brother, top Right, mothers baby sister. Picture: bottom Left, my mothers oldest sister (helped me with my mother). Bottom Middle, my grandmother. Bottom Right, my mother's second oldest sister (filled in for my older aunt with my mother)

My mother and I had a tumultuous relationship a great deal of my childhood, but there were good times that are memorable. I remember how special my mother made Christmas. It was my mother's favorite time of the year. She would always lay out my presents as if Santa just came and set them out for me. During that time, I guess wrapping gifts was too expensive or maybe it was just that she liked seeing my face light up when I came down the stairs.

I honestly didn't know that other families didn't lay their kids' gifts out, because that's what we did. I thought that was normal for everyone. When our kids came, however, my husband would not hear of just laying our kids toys out. He was raised in a family that considered wrapping gifts as part of the excitement, getting to watch his family open their gifts. They saw the excitement on each person's face, when their gifts were opened by the receiving person.

At the beginning of our parenthood, we did both, but eventually I would succumb to his tradition. Christmas was when I saw my mother happiest for the longest period. It was a guarantee that my mother would be in a perfectly happy mood all day on Christmas. It ultimately became my favorite time of the year, too.

I clearly remember Thanksgiving 1990. My mother had agreed to have Thanksgiving at our house. Usually, she would spend Thanksgiving with friends after she and George divorced.

It was a nice, crisp, sunshiny fall day. I noticed after my mother arrived; she laid on the sofa and remained there. Usually, she would be in the kitchen trying to figure out what was cooking. Finally, I asked her if she was all right. She said that she had a headache. When I asked if she could eat, she said she would give it a try. I asked how long she had a headache, and she responded that it suddenly came on her. Then I asked how long had she had a headache, and she said for a couple of weeks. I told her to make an appointment to see the doctor. She had no fever, no nausea or vomiting, and her blood pressure was slightly elevated. She was hypertensive (high blood pressure) but was being treated for it.

My mother ate some food, but not much. She went home following dinner because she still had a headache. I checked on her the next day following the holiday, and she felt better, but kept getting headaches. I asked her to go to the emergency room, but she said she had made an appointment for Monday afternoon. I urged her to, please keep that appointment.

Monday came, and my mother went to work. That morning I received a call from my aunt, who said, "Your mother was rushed to the hospital after passing out at work." I was working at another hospital not far away. When I arrived at the hospital, I was met by my aunt. When I asked her what had happened, she didn't know any more than she had told me over the phone.

I went into panic mode. I tried to open the door where they had taken my mother, but the door was locked. I asked the lady behind the information desk to open the door. She responded that she couldn't, but she would call the ER staff to see if someone could come out to talk with me.

When the attending physician came out, he said he was discharging my mother with a prescription for new blood pressure medication. I told the doctor her headaches had been coming and going for two weeks with sudden onsets. The doctor insisted that he couldn't find anything more than high blood pressure. He then walked back to where my mother was. I told my aunt they only found high blood pressure, but I felt strongly it might be something else. I wanted them to do a CAT scan or an x-ray. I tried to open the door to get back into the room in the back again, but again it was locked. In my frustration, I began to kick the door as hard as I could. The lady behind the information desk said, "Miss, you can't do that." I said, "Well let me back there with my mother." She opened the door, and I rushed back to where my mother was. When I got back there, of course, they were expecting me because, the lady at the information desk had warned them I was on the way back. The doctor that I had spoken to earlier had left for the day. There was another doctor attending to my mother. I tried to calm down in front of my mother, but I'm sure she could see the fright on my face. I asked the doctor to, please do a C.T. Scan because I felt it was something more wrong with my mother than hypertension. That was something I probably felt from the Holy Spirit. I told her of the spells; I had been told my mother had when she was young. That according to her the headaches had sudden onsets and were excruciating. Maybe they could be contributing to her sometimes erratic behavior.

The doctor agreed to do a C.T. Scan while I waited in the waiting room with my aunt. In about twenty minutes, this time the doctor called me back behind the locked door into the room where my mother was. As I listened to the words that came out of the doctor's mouth, I suddenly went into a state of shock. The doctor's words were, "Your mother has (what appears to be) three malignant brain tumors (cancerous) that are fairly large, and it appears these tumors are not the primary site. Meaning that if they are cancerous, they came or originated from some other area in the body, which means they had spread from some other place to her brain.

My heart dropped. My mother was looking at my face to see if she needed to panic. I put on as brave a face as I could. I told my mother that it was going to be all right. She said ok. They wanted to admit my mother but, I knew her diagnosis was serious, and I would need to be there as often as she needed; so I had my mother transferred to the hospital where I worked. That turned out to be a great decision (Spirit led). While I worked, I could go see my mother on my lunch hour and breaks. When she had radiation, I would pick her up after work and take her home. Also, as time progressed, I would visit her whenever she was in the hospital and still be able to go to work.

After my mother's initial diagnosis, the doctors needed to confirm the malignancy (cancer). The day she had a brain biopsy. I went to the room where the biopsy was to be done. As I stood outside the door, I could hear my mother screaming, "Ouch, ouch, ouch." When they continued, she would scream, "I said ouch." The sound of that broke my heart. Even though I had to laugh at my mother because she thought if she said ouch they would stop. Finally, they were finished, and I waited for her to come out so I could accompany her back to her room. If they gave her any anesthesia it didn't work; or maybe they hadn't given her any. All I know is it sounded like they were doing a brain biopsy on my mother's brain without any anesthesia, and she was suffering. I loved my mother no matter what! She was my only connection to this world, and I didn't want to lose her.

In a few days, my mother's diagnosis was confirmed. My mother had lung cancer with metastasis to the brain. My mother was told that she had a choice of radiation and chemotherapy, but no surgery. After a few days, the doctors told me the tumors had been there a very long time, and in order to buy her some time they needed to give her both chemo and radiation, but her diagnosis was terminal. I couldn't bring myself to tell my mother that she was going to die. I couldn't even stand the thought myself—so I went into protective mode, when the doctors talked to my mother she looked to me to explain, verify or challenge what they were saying. I tried with all my being to muster up hope. I tried for her. I tried to give her hope, but I'm not sure if I was successful.

I didn't want to talk to my mother or anyone else about her dying. I was in shock; the thought of my mother not being in my life anymore was foreign to me. The day I got my mother's diagnosis; I went directly to the liquor store and bought a fifth of bourbon and drank almost the whole bottle that night. I numbed the pain of losing my mother, but part of me wanted to let her know how I was hurting inside about my whole life.

I began to lose my focus at work, so I talked to my supervisor. I shared my mother's plight with her and how I need to speak to a counselor. She sent me to a counselor on site. I began to share my life story and how I needed to talk to my mother about my feelings before she died. I wanted her to know how much she had hurt me. I wanted to know if she was sorry for all the hurt and pain she caused me. The counselor told me that I was clinically depressed and had been for a while, talking to my mother may help me.

I thought about what the counselor said. I was scared to talk to my mother because of all the times I had tried to talk to her about my hurt and her negative reaction. She would say I was crazy or that I was the one who needed help, not her. She'd say I was too sensitive, that I thought she was a monster and that she hoped I would be a better mother to my kids. All of those comments was coated with a hint of sarcasm. She'd say, "What you need is a best friend to talk to because I can't be your best friend."

I knew the counselor was right, but because of fear and the fact that I thought of my mother dying, I felt she has enough to worry about just dealing with that. I can somehow live with my pain, and live with it I did.

What I desperately needed my mother to tell me was that I know I hurt you, I was not such a good mother, but I tried. I did not mean to hurt you, and I am so sorry, please forgive me, please, my baby, forgive me for how much pain I caused you. I never stopped loving you and I never will. But that did not happen.

I used to think when I was growing up that if my mother died, then she would go to heaven and surely she would be sorry for what she did to me. Certainly, she would be a different person than she was on earth and all things between us would finally be perfect. I could hug her and kiss her all day and her love for me would never be in question again.

I wanted that to happen someday so badly, and I believed then, and I still believe today, that someday it will truly happen

CHAPTER 7

THE SECOND DEATH

My mother's friends gave her a birthday party in August of 1989. She turned fifty-six years old. By this time, I had been married for several years, and our children were ten and twelve years old. My husband and I had good careers, and we were looking to buy our third home, a bigger home, our last home.

I did not attend my mother's birthday party. By that time, I was not hanging around my mother too much because she was drinking very heavily. I didn't want to see my mother drunk, not one more time. I did not know that my mother had stopped drinking because the chemo didn't agree with her stomach, so she couldn't drink.

All during the week and on weekends my mother drank I know that because, I would call her at least three to four times a week, and she would usually be drunk. I did not attend her party because; I just did not want to see her drunk. I did not want to embarrass her by leaving early, in case she was drunk when I got there. I was sick and tired of being sick and tired of what had become of my mother's life. I felt by then that she would never stop drinking and I had tried everything I could. I talked to her, begged, and pleaded with her to stop, but our talks usually ended with us being angry at each other.

Another thing that hurt me very much is that my mother and I would disagree and depending on how vehemently we disagreed, she may not speak to me for months. I learned to let her cool off, and when it just did not make sense to me that we were not speaking for weeks, I would call her. We would usually be able to talk, but she would remain cold in her tone with me for what might be days after that. Until she was ready to speak to me again, we did not talk. At that time, I did not know that would be my mother's last birthday party. After my mother had died, I regretted not going to her party.

I remember before my grandfather got sick; she was not speaking to me. I don't remember why, but it wasn't until my grandfather was on his deathbed that she began to speak to me again. Another time, when she was not speaking to me, I had gone on a fad diet and had lost forty pounds. Not too long after losing the weight, she told me she did not want me to get pregnant with my daughter so soon after my son was born. I went over to her house after maybe three months of not seeing her, and we had just started to speak again. I stayed about an hour. She walked me to my car, and not one time in that whole hour did she say anything about my very noticeable weight loss. That was just mean. I remember thinking, how mean and unlovable she could be to me sometimes. It hurt that she was sometimes so blatantly unkind to me. Did she think I would not notice, or was she just letting me know how she could so easily turn her love on and off toward me. It was during those times I would feel that I loved my mother because she is my mother, but sometimes I really disliked her a lot. That was another feeling that I carried throughout my life because it never changed.

When my mother began her daily radiation treatments her oldest sister who had retired helped me with my mother a lot. She was always a "take charge" person in the family. When I told her of my mother's condition, she did not ask for my permission, she just stepped right in and helped me. I did not have to ask for her help. She was always "Johnny on the spot" in everything she did. She kept up with my mother's appointments and would let me know when she needed me to take her and pick her up from her treatments.

My mother's second oldest sister would also help out when my oldest aunt could not, and I was at work. I appreciated her help as well. Most of my mother's siblings were there when I needed them, but no one helped as much as my oldest aunt. She was an angel sent by God.

My mother lost her hair during her radiation treatments because they were radiating her head. Usually, radiation does not take out your hair but chemotherapy does. I thought my mother would wear a wig, but she said, "I'm not wearing a wig. Bald heads are the style." She was a bit ahead of her time because in the 21st century bald is in for men and women, but not so much in 1989.

There were many treatments, radiation and chemotherapy, doctor's appointments, and hospitalizations. All the while my mother was growing weaker and more tired with each episode. I so wanted to talk to her about my feelings, about the way she treated and hurt me. I did not want to have regrets after she died. I hoped she would bring it up, but she didn't.

I could not talk about her dying. She would say, "If anything happens to me… and I would cut her off and say, nothing is going to happen to you." All the while, my heart was crushing because I knew what was going to happen. When I would say something to her like if things don't go well… She would cut me off the same way if she did not want to talk about it. She would say, "I don't want to think or talk about that right now." That is how we communicated with each other from 1989 to 1991.

Due to her weakness and pain, she had to decide what to do about her living arrangements. Often my mother would act like she was in denial, and she was. The social worker working on her case wanted to know my mother's plans for living arrangements. My mother said, "I'll be alright in my home." No matter what the social worker or I said, my mother had the same response. Finally, I had to be firm with my mother because they also wanted to start her on morphine. I told my mother these are your only choices, either you can come and live with us, we will have to move in with you, or you will have to go to a nursing home. She said, "I'm not going to a nursing home that's out of the question, and I don't want your life interfered with."

So we decided that if we could find someone to live with her and take care of her, then she could stay in her home. She wanted to do that. My aunt checked on her during the day, and I checked on her every evening after work. My mother's baby sister found my mother a live-in caretaker (God found that caretaker) because she was perfect for my mother. My mother liked her, and she took good care of my mother. She was the only one we interviewed, and she was perfect for the job.

On the weekends, my family would chip in with me, and share spending the night with my mother, so the caregiver could have the weekends off. Even then, my mother found the opportunity to embarrass me during her illness. I was trying to take care of my mother and was making decisions for her toward the end of her illness. Once I made a decision that I forgot to tell my mother about. When I went over to her house after work, she had a friend visiting her. She had found out about the decision I had made for her that day. As soon as I walked through the door, my mother yelled, "How dare you make decisions for me." I knew what she was referring to, but as usual I looked at her friend, to see if she was looking at me being yelled at again. She was, and as usual I was embarrassed.

I learned from nursing school that you help the patient, but always get them to participate so they would not feel that their independence is gone. I knew that, but this was my mother, and I wanted to take all the stress off of her. I wanted to take care of her. Taking care of my mother for one last time would be satisfying for me. I said I was sorry, and I understood what she was saying. I was still embarrassed just the same.

When my mother would get sick, and I would advise her on what to do, She would say: "That is why I sent you to nursing school, so you could take care of me." She would just laugh. She would also say that jokingly to her friends sometimes. Of course, I did not see the humor in that and even though I laughed, I remembered back to the time when she said she did not have any money to send me to school. I would say under my breath, especially when she had been drinking, "you did not send me to school and had it not been for God's mercy and grace, you would have to go to the doctor like the rest of society."

I watched as my mother's condition deteriorated month after month. I remember when my mother was first diagnosed, how I got into the hospital bed with her, and she hugged me so tightly. That made me feel loved, and I hugged her back. When my mother hugged me, she had the best hugs because they were tight, and I felt secure. There should have been more hugs throughout the years, but that day, we both held on to each other tightly.

Toward the end, while sitting with my mother after spending the night with her that weekend, she said to me, "You know, everything you said was true." I asked her what was true. She never answered the question and just changed the subject.

There were times during my mother's illness when I would get angry that I had to sacrifice time with my family in order to take care of her. At times I felt, "Why should I give you time that I should be spending with my family, when you didn't give me time when I needed you. Why do I have to show you love now; when your love for me was always questionable? Just because you are my mother, I have to take care of you now that you are sick, but where were you all those times that I needed you?" I had to try and block those feelings, otherwise I would not have been able to do anything for my mother.

The caregiver called me one night to say my mother was having a seizure. I called my mother's oldest sister and asked her to meet me there. When I got there, my mother was laying on her bed having a grand mal seizure. When my aunt got there, she asked if I wanted her to call hospice. They had just started working with her. I said yes. It took the nurse

20 minutes to get to the house, and my mother had a seizure the whole time. I called an ambulance, and when they got there, they said they could not take her to a D.C. hospital since we were in Maryland. My mother's doctor was in D.C. The ambulance attendant and paramedic helped us get my mother into my aunt's car, which was a compact car. In the process, I believe we broke her leg. She began to scream as we rushed her to the hospital, running stop signs and red lights.

We got to the hospital, and my mother was seen by a doctor and admitted. She was barely awake, but the seizure had stopped. It was late when she was admitted, so after getting her settled, we kissed her and left to go home. That was Monday night.

The next day I went to see my mother before I began work and on my break. She slept all day. On Wednesday, I went to see her several times that day, but after work, I went to see her, and my aunt who was helping me was there. She said she had been asleep during her visit. At that time, they had not taken an x-ray of her leg, but they were keeping her free from pain with morphine. We still did not know if her leg was broken. Before my aunt and I left, I said to my mother, "I love you. Do you love me?" I said it two times with no answer. The third time I shouted a little louder and to my surprise, she shouted, "Very much so." Those were the last words my mother ever spoke to me. That night, I got a call from the hospital letting me know that my mother had taken a turn for the worse, and we needed to get there quickly. I called my aunt, she called the rest of my mother's sisters, her brother and my mother's best friend. My husband, our children, and me rushed as fast as we could to the hospital.

My husband pulled up to the front of the hospital, and I jumped out. The kids stayed with him while he parked the car. I ran to the unit, and as I was passing the nurses' desk the nurse said, she did not make it. I asked the nurse when did she die, and she said five minutes ago. I ran to the room; my mother was laying in the bed partially propped up by pillows. She had the most peaceful look on her face that I had ever seen in my whole life with her. I laid on her warm chest and began to sob. "Why couldn't you wait for me to get here, Ma," I cried. "You knew I was coming?" I sobbed like a baby needing her bottle. I needed my mother, and she was gone. I kissed her, as did my husband and children when they arrived, this was the last time we saw her until the day of the funeral. I felt so alone that night and was in shock that my mother had died. How could she die and leave me here all alone? My heart was truly broken into pieces that night; I had never felt so broken in my life, until that day.

My mother's siblings and her best friend arrived at the hospital, and each one said their goodbyes. We decided to go tell my grandmother who was at home with her sister. When we walked into the house, my grandmother knew what we had come to say. I went to her first and hugged my grandmother and said my mother was gone. My grandmother had just lost her child, the first one to die. She was grieving too, but she took care to hold me and tell me how sorry she was. The comfort she had always given me was in full supply that night. She was most concerned about me even though she had just lost her child, a child who was not supposed to die before her parents. My mother was fifty-six years old, younger than I am now. I realized that my grandmother had lost her first child, and I comforted her too that night. I thought to myself; this has to be the worst day of my life. I did not know then that it was the beginning of many more sorrows.

CHAPTER 8

THE STORM BEGINS TO RAGE AGAIN.

My mother died on March 28, 1991, at an age much too young in my mind. Many family and friends attended her funeral. She was honored and remembered for her accomplishments in work, for helping others, and for being a good person. I was proud that she was remembered for the good that she had done. I just wished someone had been able to say that she was a good wife, mother and Christian.

I was very disappointed that my biological father did not attend my mother's funeral. My first stepfather attended my mother's funeral with his wife, which I did not appreciate. We did not like each other, and she did not like my mother and my mother did not like her. My second stepfather did not bother to attend my mother's funeral, nor did he offer me condolences. However, I was pleased that two of his brothers did come.

I believe my mother was a Christian, but she was a backslider. She loved the Lord, but she had allowed her life to stray from the Lord through her lifestyle. My mother prayed and believed in the Lord. By the end of her life, she realized that she had allowed her life to go down the wrong path. When my mother told me everything, I told her was true. She let me know that she understood what I had told her about drinking all those years. Drinking adversely affected her life.

My mother did take my advice on making sure that everything was in order when she died, however. After her death there was a smooth transition of all her possessions, property, and finances. She even picked out her headstone for the gravesite. I did appreciate what she had done in that regard because it took a lot of weight off me.

The weeks following my mother's funeral were a blur. Especially when I sat at the settlement table to transfer her house to the new owner. That is when I realized "this is final, I just sold my mother's house". I had to leave the settlement table before signing any paperwork. I needed to catch my breath and absorb the realization of what was about to happen. If I am about to turn over my mother's house to someone else that means she is gone, dead, and never coming back. That was just a little more than I could bear at that moment, and I needed to breathe. So I stepped out of the room to breathe some fresh air before I passed out. After a few moments, I returned and completed the transaction to transfer the property. I was very surprised by my reaction to selling my mother's house. It never occurred to me that I would feel the finality of my mother's death at that moment, but I did, and it made me very sad.

I began drinking on a regular basis a few months after the funeral had passed. My mother's death was beginning to take its toll on me emotionally. I missed my mother so much, and as people often do in grief, I began to put my mother on a pedestal. I saved her clothes and wore them. I would not give anything of hers away. I did not let anyone speak negatively about my mother. I also would only speak of the good things my mother did, said, and remembered her fondly.

I told my biological father about my mother's death, but he said he could not come to the funeral because he had a previous engagement. All I could think is "couldn't he take a break?" Later my father tried to tell me about my mother's spells long ago, and he knew something was wrong with her. I cut him off immediately and said "Don't say bad things about my mother because I don't want to hear it!" How dare you have another engagement when the mother of your child has just died? Then speak negatively about her! He had the nerve to continue to say something negative about her, and I slammed the phone down and did not speak to him for months after that.

None of the fathers in my life cared enough about me to come to my mother's funeral or to support me. I felt very alone during this time in my life. Had it not been for my family on my mother's side, I would have felt even more abandoned. I believed that the men in my mother's life did not care for either one of us. That is a cold hard fact to have to face in an hour when you are most vulnerable. So, there I was on the day of my mother's death, without one parent left to comfort me. The feeling was awful! Total abandonment and rejection were what I felt that day. I'll never forget or be able to erase the pain of that day in my life.

I was able to get through the holidays following my mother's death fairly well, but that Thanksgiving after my mother passed was difficult. We had been having dinner for the past few years together on Thanksgiving. Suddenly, the Thanksgiving after her death, I realized my family, and I had nowhere to go. All my mother's brothers and sisters had their families they shared Thanksgiving with, I didn't want to tell anyone how I was feeling about not having someplace to go. I didn't even have the energy or frame of mind to fix dinner for my family that year.

My mother's baby sister invited my family and me to have dinner with her family the year after my family spent Thanksgiving alone. It reminded me that I still had a family without my mother. I realized that my mother was my only connection to the people I called my family, aunts, uncles, grandparents, and cousins for my whole life. Without her, I felt unconnected to my family. Again, I was the only one in my family who not only lost fathers, but now, I had lost my mother. She was my connection to my whole family. I had never felt that feeling before in my whole life, and it was not a comfortable place to be. It felt horrible!

Four years after my mother's death, my mother's oldest sister, the one who was such a big help during my mother's illness, died. She had pancreatic cancer. My aunt asked me when she was preparing for her death what I regretted not doing most before my mother died. I told her it was that we did not talk about her impending death with each other. It was also that we did not discuss our hearts with each other and did not make amends. My aunt took that information to heart. Before she died, we as a family gathered around her bedside one by one. We told her what we would miss most about her, and she told us what she loved most about us. It was a very emotional time as we each went into her room one by one, and each took our turn, talking and listening to her. There was a lot of crying that day in her home, yet it was so cathartic. It made each of us feel good to hear how we each had made a difference in her life.

After we all had taken our turn, we gathered around her bedside and sang hymns. We were crying, but I know for me, I had ambivalent feelings. I felt good that I had said good things about our relationship, and I felt good that she loved and appreciated the difference I made in her life. The truth is, I was going to miss the hell out of my aunt. She was always the strong one in our family. She was bossy but organized and emphatic about what we should do about any circumstance. She had a "take-charge" personality. We did not always know what to do, but we knew our aunt did, so we would always go to her for direction. Even my grandparents went to her if they felt they needed direction. I was going to miss her for that, and I still do.

$\mathscr{C}$HAPTER 9

WHAT HAPPENED TO ME?

Valencia and cousin

Shortly after my mother's death, I tried to carry on as usual with working, taking care of my husband and kids, but sadness filled my heart. I began to drink more as I thought about my mother, and how she would still be here, if she had listened to me when I asked her to stop drinking. My heart and soul ached because I did not have a better childhood and a better relationship with my mother. I loved her so much; did she love me as much as I loved her? I wondered why we could not talk about where our relationship went wrong, and could it be mended? Why did my mother not love me enough to stop drinking and why couldn't she stop hurting me?

I needed answers. But the only one who could answer those questions was my mother, and she was gone. I wondered if I would hurt like this for the rest of my life. Was my mother sorry for the way she treated me while she lived? Why could she not recognize how sad she made me and at least apologize, but she never did. That hurt more than anything did, so I drank to mask my pain. I did not want to ever feel sadness anymore because it hurts too much. Whenever I drank, I drank until I did not care what my life with my mother was like, or my life without her in it.

There were also times when I felt if I died I would go to be with my mother and everything would be perfect. She would love me totally and apologize to me for all the pain she caused in my life. So I guess subconsciously I was trying to commit suicide. All I wanted was to rest in my mother's arms and hear her say, "Baby, I love you, I always have, and I always will. Please forgive me for what I did to you. I'm so sorry I hurt you."

I never heard her say that, so I drank and when I did, I did not care if I wasn't loved by anyone. Because when I drank I felt, my husband and kids did not love me either. So what in hell did I have to lose. Maybe if I lost myself, I would gain my mother.

What I did not realize until fifteen years later (after drinking heavily), was that during all of my sadness, pain, depression, grief, self-absorption, and self-pity, I had become an alcoholic. My kids were angry with me, and my husband was saddened and did not know how to help me.

I drank from sun up to sun down on the weekends, until I passed out. During the week, I drank after work until I passed out at night. I would try to meet my obligations, and continued to do that for years, but towards the end of the fifteen years, I became very isolated. All I wanted to do was drink, and I would stay at home on the weekends and do just that.

My husband called an intervention with my three aunts present. I was shocked that I hadn't hidden my condition from my family very well. Even my grandmother would call me and minister to me, but she would only tell me that God loved me, and He wanted me to take control of my life and always keep Him first in my life. She never mentioned the alcohol, and I did not know she was talking about that. The devil had convinced me that I had fooled everyone.

When anyone would call me on the phone, I would always answer the phone and thought I was talking normally, but often my speech would be slurred. Our children were on their own by this time, but they would not come around much. I just thought; that was the way grown kids acted toward their parents. It never dawned on me that I did the same thing to my mother, because she was drinking, and I did not want to be around her.

I was beginning to realize after my intervention that maybe I needed to cut back on drinking. My husband and I went to my psychiatrist that I had been seeing since my mother died who gave me medication to help me stop drinking. As I look back on that day, I was drunk at the doctor's office. I had begun to slip because, before that day, I would never have let anyone see me drunk but my husband. The medication the doctor gave me did not help one bit. I was hooked by then, and I drank without thinking about it.

During this fifteen-year period, I discovered I was diabetic. Even taking medication for diabetes, I continued to drink. When my family would come to my house, and I was drinking, they would say, "You shouldn't be drinking while you are taking medication for diabetes, should you?" I would say, "Oh I'm fine," knowing they were right, but I did not stop drinking. There were times while drinking I would fall. Once I fell down the stairs in my home, and it took about fifteen minutes before I was able to get up. Another time, I fell over our doggie gate we had put in place to keep our dog from roaming all over the house. When I fell, I broke my ankle and had to crawl on the floor and pull the phone down off the wall in order to call my husband. Even my dog was concerned because she kept licking me while I lay on the floor.

When my husband rushed home from work, which was forty-five minutes away, I was still lying on the floor drunk and with my dog who had kept me company while I waited for him. My husband rushed me to the hospital, and they x-rayed and stabilized my ankle until I was able to go to surgery. My surgery consisted of putting a plate in my ankle with eight screws to stabilize it. It's been eleven years since my ankle surgery, and I still have the plate and screws in my ankle.

By this time in my drinking, I was hiding things from my children. I felt like they hated me, so why not keep doing what I am doing. The truth is, I was embarrassed to let them know how far out of control my drinking had become.

My husband and I began to argue. We have not argued much in our lives. My husband is a peaceful man, and I do not like arguing ever since my parents began doing it. We did argue, but it was not often. During my drinking years, especially toward the end, we were arguing quite a bit. He had less patience with me but would not always say it. He would just lose his temper with me more often. My husband told me he was worried that I was drinking too much, and appeasing him; I agreed to go to my church to see if I could get help. Drunk again, my husband took me to see one of our ministers. To my surprise, she agreed to help me.

She began coming to see me at my house. I honestly didn't care what condition I was in when the minister came. Most of the time I was intoxicated and really did not care about being that way. I would meet the minister in my pajamas and refused to put on clothes. By this time, I did not care how I looked, smelled or anything. All I wanted was for the meeting to be over so I could go back to my drinking. There was a couple of times that I drank while the minister was there. She really did not like that much and let me know, but I would continue until she told me if I was going to drink while she was there she was not coming back; so I had to stop doing it around her. I was beginning to be happy to see her and did not want her to stop coming to see me. I felt she cared.

She would make me mad sometimes because she told me that I needed help. I did not want to hear that because she was talking about me going to an inpatient facility. I told her on many occasions that I did not need help so bad that I had to leave my home to get help. I was not going to spend the night anywhere but at my house. For one whole year after, the minister told me I needed to go to an inpatient facility. I kept saying no I am not going, often with much anger. She dealt with my rudeness, cursing, and my condition for over one year and continued to come back week after week.

One night I had a dream that I woke up one morning, and I was in jail. When I inquired why I was there, the guard said, "Don't you remember, you killed your husband?" I was so scared that my husband was dead first of all and that I had killed him. Then I realized I was going to jail for the rest of my life, and I didn't even remember what happened. That dream woke me up in sheer terror.

I was talking to the minister helping me, and I was telling her something. She said, "You told me that already." I asked her when did I tell her, and she said when you called me at 2 a.m. this morning. "Oh my God, this morning," Oh my God, I called you at 2 a.m. I gasped, she said yes you did. I apologized profusely, and though she forgave me, I realized then, that I did need help. The minister said, "If you don't remember who you called, you don't remember what you said."

The thought of that was frightening! I always prided myself in keeping others' secrets and only telling a few people my secrets. What if I called someone and told him or her my innermost secrets or told them someone else's secret that I had sworn to keep. Remember, I was raised in a pastor's home, and I was used to hiding secrets, even if they were good.

Losing my freedom for killing anyone was most frightening. I did not drink and drive, but what If I did get in the car, drunk, and accidently kill someone in the street and end up in jail. I would be remorseful forever, but I would also be in jail forever. My life would be ruined. I thought to myself; I need to stop this now! The next day my grandmother called me and said, "If you don't stop drinking, you are going to lose your husband." My heart sunk at the thought of that! For the first time, I realized my grandmother knew I had been drinking heavily. I did not say a word to anyone about my revelations, but the next time the minister came to my house, I indicated that I would look into a facility. I explained why I had come to that conclusion, and I saw happiness in the minister's face. I could see that she was grateful for a positive answer to her prayers. She inquired almost daily about my research in finding a recovery house.

My male cousin, the one I grew up with, had been in a treatment facility in D.C. for drug addiction. I called him, and he made a call to that facility, and the next thing you know, he got me in that facility. That turned out to be one of the best decisions I ever made. It was almost summer, and since I was now working in the school system, I could go over the summer break, and no one but my family would know.

I had left the operating room ten years prior to my heavy drinking due to severe arthritis in my knees. It had become difficult to get around the OR in a hurry the way I used to get around. The pain had become unbearable, so I had to make a job change. I worked in the school system as a school nurse and enjoyed the slower pace and not having to stand on my feet for so long as in the OR.

Everyone in my family was happy that I had decided to go into a facility, and they commented on how brave I was to go. I did not think I was so brave. I was scared to death because I did not know what to expect. I did not want to leave my husband, and the closer I got to the time to go, I was very emotional, as was my husband. I did not want to lose him. He was there for me the whole time, and I loved him very much for not leaving me. I wanted to give him a better wife, and he told me that he wanted his wife back. So for my sake, my husband, children, and my grandmother's sake, I went into treatment for twenty-eight days, and my life has never been the same since that day.

10 years post treatment.

CHAPTER 10

WHAT AN EXPERIENCE

When I decided to go into a treatment facility, I did not know what to expect. The only thing I knew was I would not be allowed to drink. Other than not being allowed to drink, everything else came as a complete surprise to me.

When I entered the center, my husband had to drop me off in the lobby, and someone from the facility came to meet us. I did not know that that was the last time I would see my husband for twenty-eight days. I did not know that I would not be able to talk to him either. When it was time to go, my husband said he'd call me, and my escort said, "She won't be allowed to receive or make calls. You also won't be able to visit her." My husband and I were sad about that information, and I began to cry. When I got myself together, I kissed my husband goodbye and said I'll see you soon.

My escort took me in the elevator to a place upstairs in the building. Immediately a woman came in and introduced herself to me. She said she would have to search my bags. What? She took me to my room, which had two sets of bunk beds. She seemed like a nice person, but I felt like a prisoner. She said you'll be sleeping on the top bunk. I had severe arthritis. "How in the world am I going to get up on that top bunk," I asked. She said, "You might be able to switch with one of the other ladies in the room." Oh, good I thought. To my surprise, no one wanted to switch with me, so I had to climb my big butt with arthritic knees up to the top bunk. I suddenly became scared to be in this place. No one was nice enough to understand my plight and switch with me. They were young ladies, and I was fifty-two years old.

God gave me strength to try to look beyond my situation and see that I had to make the best of this thing because I was doing it for a good cause. I went into what I call a fog after that. I had to decide to make this thing work, and maybe be a little tough while I'm at it.

The meals were a little different. We had to sit at a table with five to a table. We had to wait until the woman in the kitchen said we could eat. When she said we could eat, we had to line up and go get our food. The meal was full of starchy foods, like rice, beans, macaroni, and cheese, potatoes, meat, and vegetables. There would always be more starchy foods than anything else. The girls I sat with at the table seemed nice enough. They introduced themselves and told me what I had to do concerning the meal. We were not allowed to look out of the window, watch T.V., or read anything. I am a news buff, and the thought of not knowing what's going on in my world was excruciating.

Each morning we had to go for a long walk around the area where we were. The facility was located in Adams Morgan, which is near Howard University. The walk was very long, maybe two to three miles, and my knees hurt. The ankle I broke swelled every day. I tried to get out of the walk, but they would not let me. I think they did not believe me when I said I was in pain, but they soon saw that my ankle was swelling. They told me to sit down in the park (called Malcolm X) when we got to it, which I did, but it only helped a little. I prayed every day. I walked asking Jesus to help me through my daily walks and the pain in my knees and ankle. Each day I knew God was with me because I made it through, never without pain but always with enough stamina to get to the end.

We had group meetings every day twice a day, and we would sing at morning group an uplifting gospel song. That was fun to me because music makes me happy, so I looked forward to singing. The meeting allowed me to learn about the other residents in the facility. I felt that I came from a fairly, middle class family and certainly my husband, and I had created a middle-class life for ourselves. I grew up in the church. I was not perfect, or better than anyone else, but I tried my best to stay out of trouble all my life and for the most part had, until the drinking. I was successful. I have never been arrested, nor have I been to jail. Suddenly, for the first time in my life, I sat in group meetings with criminals, prostitutes, drug addicts, dealers and a murderer. People who had been to jail throughout their whole lives. One man had been in jail for fifteen years for murder.

Wow, I don't know what I expected, but the thought of being in the presence of these residents for any length of time was amazing to me as well as intimidating. We had to tell our stories and as time went on I became friends with the residents. As I moved on in the program, I moved from thinking I don't belong here, to realizing I was just like them in that what I had was an addiction and so did they. The difference between us was that I hid my mess a little better and never got caught. We were all addicts of one sort or another and needed help. We made bad choices and ended up where we were.

There was a time when we were in our group and this young boy (around sixteen years old), who always liked to dominate our conversations. Every other word that came out of his mouth was a curse word which caused an outburst in me. I had had enough of his always manipulating the conversations, and I was even more disgusted with his foul mouth.

After about the fifth "MF" had come out of his mouth, I yelled across the room, you don't respect women do you? The group members chuckled, but there wasn't anything funny except I busted him out in front of twenty-five people. He gasped and asked, "Why do you say that?" I said, "I am old enough to be your grandmother, and yet you sit here in front of me and all these other women and cuss like we are invisible. I am not invisible, and I don't appreciate your filthy mouth!" Everyone clapped, but I was angry at this disrespectful, pipsqueak. The counselor, who was a male, said to him, "She's right man, you need to clean up your language." From that day on, he cursed less., If he slipped, he would apologize to me. I guess that was the best I was going to get out of him.

I began smoking cigarettes my first day in college, probably because of fear of being on my own and in a strange environment. That continued into my adult life. In the facility I went to, we were locked in the center. Only the staff could come and go. As I said, I did not know what to expect before getting there. I soon found out that I would only be able to smoke three cigarettes a day. I was a pack a day smoker for years. What was I going to do? I wanted to leave the minute I found out those were the conditions. Locked inside a building, not being able to look out of the window, watch T.V. or read. Blinds closed 24/7. They would tell you when you could go to bed, wake up, wash your clothes. Plus we had chores we could not refuse to do. I had gotten to the point in my life where I hired someone to clean my house, and now I have to clean the toilets! There were so many times in the beginning that I wanted to leave, and I could have, but was always talked out of it by the residents or counselors. One time, while we were on the roof smoking, someone threw something in an attempt to hit someone on the ground. That was the end of our smoke break. I had just lit my cigarette. I almost became a murderer that day, but God is good. The thing I dreaded the most had happened. I had lost my freedom. There were incidents like this happening during my twenty-eight day stay at the facility, but I learned, if I ever get out of this prison, I would never be back, never!

I eventually was able to get a low bunk bed, as people had made their twenty-eight days and moved on. Some went to another facility if they needed additional help or had nowhere else to go. And others like me went home. Thank God!

I learned that we all have problems, but we have to face our problems head on and not drink, drug, or criminalize our way to a solution. When I had emotional pain, I learned to drink so I wouldn't feel the pain so much. I didn't want to feel the pain I had felt my whole life anymore, and drinking had become my way of not feeling. I learned I had to allow myself to feel the pain, in order to deal with it, and learn to forgive those who hurt me in order to heal. If I did not do that, I would never get better.

After being there a couple of weeks, I spoke to one of the counselors and told her, I couldn't stop feeling the pain of how my mother hurt me. She set up a meeting with one of the girls who was about to graduate from the program, and the girl and I role played. She was my mother, and I had to say what I would tell my mother if she were here. We got very involved in the role play, and by the end, I was on the road to my healing.

When we role played, at times, I was surprised at what the girl's answers would be to my questions, as if my mother was answering the questions through her. I asked the girl playing my mother, why she hurt me, and she said, she was hurting herself and did not know how to be my mother. She said she was so sorry she hurt me, and if she had it to do again, she would do everything differently and make sure that she made me aware of how much she loved me. She said she was selfish and self-centered and did not know how to love me. I cried and cried because that is what I wanted to hear my mother say, "I always loved you more than you know, and I am so sorry I hurt you. Please forgive me." That is what the girl said and that made a difference in the way I saw my mother. I felt sorry for her that she did not know how to love me because of her pain. That was my turning point, and I felt I could make it through the program.

I graduated and was recognized as the one in my class with the most growth during my twenty-eight days. I was asked to give the graduation speech for my class, and it was a very funny and moving speech. I talked about the day with the cigarette incident in my speech. When we had to cut our break short, and I hadn't finished my smoke, I got angry and told the counselor. I was never coming back, here again, when I'm able to get out of here. I thought he would change his mind, and let us smoke, in spite of what someone had stupidly done. To my surprise, the counselor said, "Good, I don't want to see you back here." My feelings were hurt. I thought well that was not nice for him to say. Never mind I had just said something that was not nice to him. He said, "I don't care if you're mad either." I was fuming. Isn't that stupid? I was boiling mad because my counselor wouldn't let me kill myself by smoking, and thought he would care if I insulted him for not allowing me to do so.

When I finished the program, and was contemplating writing the speech, I realized that the reason the counselor said what he said to me. He was wishing me success and hoped I would not drink again so I would not have to come back. When I realized that was what he meant, I had to laugh. What I thought was being mean was a blessing he was pronouncing on me. When I read that part of my speech, I looked at him, and he gave me a thumbs up, as if to say, you got it. As I look back even today at that graduation day and my speech, I still smile.

My eighty-nine-year-old grandmother attended my graduation, as did my husband, my aunts, and the minister who helped me. I left treatment that day in July with my husband, and we were so happy that our separation was over. We couldn't stop loving on each other as we had never been separated for more than two days since we were married. I have been sober for eleven- and-one-half years. Hallelujah!

Only God could have set me free! The road to sobriety was hard. I had to allow myself to feel so much pain and not drink to that pain. I had to learn to forgive those who hurt me, and I had to reaffirm my relationship with my husband and kids. I realized many truths about my family, kids and husband that I was not aware of before entering that treatment facility. I discovered those truths when I got sober, and I understood that I had caused a lot of pain in my family. Once I became aware of what those truths were, I had to make amends.

$\mathcal{C}$HAPTER *11*

MY REVELATIONS

I went home after my graduation from the treatment center. I was afraid because I did not know what I would do without the support of my counselors and friends from the center if I wanted to drink. With each day, I was able to say I choose not to drink today. It is true that you have to take one day at a time, and you are more conscious of that each day you wake up.

The first significant thing that happened after leaving the facility involved my daughter. She had been dating her boyfriend for several months prior to my treatment and told me she was pregnant. She was an adult, had graduated from college, was working, and was living on her own. But I had always told her not to get pregnant before marriage. I was devastated! She seemed to be ok about it and stated they were going to get married before the baby was born. That sort of made me feel a little better, but I wasn't sure about her choice for her husband. I asked her if she loved the guy and if he loved her? Her answer to both questions was affirmative. She said she wanted to keep the baby, which I was glad about, but my feelings about her fiancé bothered me a bit. There was nothing I could put my finger on that made me somewhat concerned, but he just did not seem to be as in love with her as I thought he should be. My husband and I gave them our blessing, and we immediately began planning their wedding.

My daughter and her fiancés wedding kept me busy and kept my mind off of drinking, we only had three months to get it done. My concerns about her fiancé began to spark on their wedding day. After the ceremony, while waiting for pictures to be taken by the photographer, her new husband wanted to spend time with his friends who had come to the wedding rather than his new bride. My daughter was upset about that, and I had to say something to her husband about the proper behavior of couples on their wedding day.

After the couple had gone on their honeymoon to Puerto Vallarta, they began their life together and made plans for their soon arrival.

I had been thinking about going back to school to get my degree in counseling. My interest was grief counseling, as I wanted to help others get over losing a loved one. I found a school offering that major and I began classes online from a university located in Alabama. Not long after finishing my first class, my beautiful grandson was born. He was so precious to my husband and me, and it gave me great joy to be able to take care of him in the evenings, while his mother went to paralegal school at Georgetown University.

Things did not work out with my daughter and her husband and they eventually divorced after two years of marriage. I was right about him. It turned out that he only wanted to hang out with his friends, drink, and smoke marijuana. When he put his hands on her in a violent, physical way, she got smart and out of a relationship that was not going anywhere.

I do not condone divorce, but when a man is violent against his wife, I was always taught that if he does it once, he will do it again. I taught her that, too.

My son was married to someone I did not particularly care for at the time. She was bossy, and she did not like me much either. We had a run in when she and my son were dating. She ignored my concerns, and led my son away from his family, which I felt was vindictive because of the relationship we had while they were dating.

She and my son divorced after being married for only five years. Now he's married to a woman that I love. My son and his wife also have a beautiful baby boy whom I love very much. They had their second child in May of 2013, a beautiful baby girl.

The next significant thing that happened after completing my treatment was my biological father was diagnosed with lung cancer. My father and I never resolved our problems of the past, and I really did not want to take care of him in any way during his illness. He was living in Philadelphia where he was born and raised, and I lived in Maryland. I was sitting in my house one day thinking about him, and the Lord said to me, "Honor thy father and thy mother." I had honored my mother by taking care of her even though she did not do a great job of taking care of me. My father had done much less than my mother had done for me, and I did not feel obligated to care for him. But God said, "Honor thy father."

I called my father to check on him and made a decision to do what God said, so I went to visit him. We sat and talked.

On a few more occasions, I spent time with him. When my father died, I felt that I had done what God had asked me to do. So I was happy about that. I did not, however, feel the same sadness about his passing as I did when my mother passed. What I am most sad about is my father did not make much of an effort to have a relationship with his children. Furthermore, he spent the least amount of time with me. He spent more time in the cities where his four sons were born than he ever spent with me. My sister grew up in Philadelphia where our father lived, and even though he did not see her much either, he saw her more than he saw me because I lived in Maryland.

I helped my younger brother plan his funeral and few people were in attendance. I was sad for my father who lived his life doing only what he wanted to do, with whomever he wanted to do it with at that time. In the end, he died alone.

My husband and I began to mend our relationship after our daughter's marriage; our son's divorce and my father died. All those things seemed to bombard us after my treatment.

In between those episodes, I had to attend Alcoholic Anonymous (AA). I tried to attend at least once or twice a week at first. After about a year of doing that, I did not feel that I was getting a lot out of those meetings. My higher power is God, and I felt like I was helped more when I attended church and began to spend more time with him on a daily basis. That has kept me sober. While I have nothing against AA, it just did not sustain me as much as getting intimate with God.

I learned during the first year after graduating from the treatment facility that I hurt my immediate family so much during my years of drinking. For instance, I didn't know how long my husband had been concerned about my heavy drinking, and the constant arguments we had were due to my actions and the frustration he was feeling during those years. He said he did not know how to help me, and he prayed every day, several times a day that God would help me stop drinking. He told me that he would sit in the family room at night crying (while I was upstairs in our bedroom drunk) because he felt he had lost his wife.

The revelation of my husband crying because I would not stop drinking meant he was at his wits end, My grandmother was right; I was probably on the verge of losing the love of my life. I had made drinking more important than pleasing him. Hearing what he was feeling about me and my drinking during those years, and that it was so bad that he would often cry about it, made me very sad. I wanted to make everything up to him because he could have left, but he didn't. As we talked about his feelings during this time, I fell in love with him all over again. For the first time I knew, that I had found someone who did not abandon me, who loved me even at my worst, and loved me even more at my best. Though my early years of life were not the best, my latter years were looking greater than ever. I praise God for His mercy, kindness, love, and grace through the trials of our marriage.

I learned that our daughter moved out of our house and on her own so early (much earlier than I wanted her to) because she could not stand my drinking one minute longer. She never said one word to me about that until I was sober. I found out how she felt in a very hurtful way, too. Her mother-in-law told me that she had told her that was why she left home. I learned how she felt after she was separated from her husband and her mother-in-law, and I were in a heated conversation about our children's marriage. In anger, she blurted it out to me over the phone. I was shocked to hear that from her in the heat of our conversation! When I was able to speak to my daughter about what she had told someone else that was so personal to us, I was angry.

I asked my daughter how she could do such a thing. She said she and her mother-in-law were talking and in a moment of compassion she had said, "I wish I could talk to my mother about these things. But I left home because she drank too much, and I could not stand it, nor did I want to talk to her." I felt so betrayed by my daughter and deeply hurt. Once I was able to think about what my daughter had done, I realized that I caused her to feel that way. It was my fault not hers, and I would have to make amends for that. I apologized profusely to my daughter and vowed that I would do what I could do to make things right again with my child. I could hardly bear the hurt that my daughter had felt from my actions.

My son continued to display frequent outbursts against me. I thought his outbursts would go away once he was not a teenager anymore. They persisted through the years, and when we had a disagreement after his son was born, I discovered that his outbursts were not only about our disagreement, but were the result of a bigger picture. His outbursts were bordering on the line of disrespect. In fact, at times, he was very disrespectful in his tone and actions towards me.

I decided to confront him regarding his disrespect towards

me. When I confronted him about being disrespectful to me, I heard for the first time that he hated the fact that I drank too much and saw me drunk. I thought as I have said before that I hid my drinking very well. I was now discovering through my son that I did not hide one thing from him. He was very angry with me about it. Again, I was very sorry that I had hurt my son so much. When he was born, he was my heart, a mother, and her son. We were very close while he was growing up, and I wanted us to be close for life. To know that I had hurt him so much broke my heart.

Wow, I suddenly realized that my drinking had affected my whole family, mainly my husband, children, and my grandmother. The four people that I love most in this world, I had caused them so much pain. I felt guilt, sadness, pain, embarrassment and so undeserving of their love, Maybe I felt what my mother felt during her life, I thought.

I knew that I had done some things very wrong, and I needed to try to make those things right again.

CHAPTER 12

COULD I HANDLE THE TRUTH?

Valencia and Husband

This book will not be noted for its professional problem-solving skills nor is it meant to diagnose any disease. This story is about my experience, and how I was able to make it through my problems. Hopefully, someone will benefit from my experience and may find that the way I was delivered from my demons may help them also to break free from theirs.

After I had stopped drinking, I realized something that scared me quite a bit. I realized that I had to feel my pain. Throughout my life, whenever I felt pain, I had to isolate myself and pretend I was not hurting. When I became an adult, when I felt the pain, I drank.

When you get sober and wish to remain sober, you must allow yourself to feel the pain, not cover it up, and not drink to the pain. That is when the real pain is realized. You can no longer hide from the pain, but you have to face it head on.

During my recovery period, I lost a very precious person, my grandmother. She died in November of 2007 at ninety-seven years old.

Just before her death, she voted for the first African-American president. She was elated about Barack Obama becoming the first Black President. That following February in 2008, she would have been ninety-eight. God allowed her to see her granddaughter get sober, and we spent a good amount of time together. My cousins and I scheduled ourselves to take care of her every Saturday, to give my youngest aunt with whom she lived with a break. I miss my grandmother a lot because we talked almost every day. She was alert, was able to get around with the assistance of a cane, and she was coherent up until the very end. Her whole life she was afraid to die and would always say, "I'm going to stay here as long as I can." But when the end came, she just went to sleep. I loved her so much!

As I stated earlier, I needed help to deal with my pain, so I sought a new counselor. In counseling, I recognized that the life I had growing up was not a normal life children have in happy homes. I had to understand that I had been abused verbally and sometimes physically by my mother.

I had to face the fact that my mother was not a good mother. She was selfish and was resentful that she and my father didn't make it. She was saddened about that, and she hated my father even though she loved him, too. Often my mother would say, "You look just like your father" and even that upset her I do believe. I also realized that my mother had emotional problems, which had gone untreated. Therefore, she didn't know how to conduct herself properly as a mother, or a woman scorned. I tried to talk her into getting help, but she wouldn't hear of it. She would always say, "You're the one who needs help, not me."

During the time I was facing my life head on, I asked my family about my mother and about some of the things she did. I had been told by my grandmother that my mother had been a problem child, and had given my grandparents many problems that concerned them as she was growing up.

My grandmother said my mother had spells when she was little. She would space out sometimes and sometimes would suddenly go off and cause disruption in the household with sudden outbursts and tearing up things. She said her behavior was often unpredictable.

I found out that I had to stay with my grandparents when I was two because my mother was emotionally unstable. When I went to live with my mother at age seven, she was more stable, but behind closed doors and with her increased drinking, she became more unstable as time went on. Since she drank mostly after work in the beginning, her unstableness was after she was away from outsiders. As her drinking escalated over the years, she became more unstable around others and me.

In therapy, I learned that my mother did love me, but didn't always know how to show it. I learned that because of my mother's pain, she would often inflict her pain on me. I believe she felt that my birth and subsequently having to take care of me caused her to miss out on the things she wanted to do in life. I also learned that my mother always felt unloved because my father broke her heart. I learned that as she was the baby girl of her family for eleven years, when her youngest sister was born, the attention my grandparents had given her those years diminished somewhat. And my mother became very jealous of her sister. She never got over that I don't think, which was evident when my mother pushed my young aunt down the stairs for no reason. That became a point of contention between them for many years.

My mother's philosophy was, "Don't do what I do, do what I say do." That made me bitter because when she treated me bad, I didn't want to hear that, and I couldn't act out the way I wanted to. So I had to stifle my feelings. That made me depressed because I couldn't express myself. That is when I began writing letters to my mother and writing poems.

My mother and I did not talk about any of this before she died, so all my revelations regarding our relationship came after her death and after my alcoholism manifested.

Once I had done an extensive amount of psychotherapy, medication therapy and with the help of my God, I was able to begin my healing process. When I faced the issues in my life and got a better understanding of the who, what, how, when, and why. When I was able to embrace my past, become comfortable in my own skin, I knew I was on my way. The process included recognizing; copings, forgiveness, faith, focus, truth, and acceptance just to mention a few characteristics needed to move forward.

ECOGNIZING:

Ecclesiastes 3:1 brought to my attention that, "To everything there is a season, a time for every purpose under heaven..."

I had to be born; I had to be born to my parents, but my home had to have a godly foundation. Regardless of who my parents were, I had to be born to them because that's the way God wanted it. I don't know why, but God decided that was the way it was to be. I had to realize that God knew what He was doing when He placed me with my parents.

God knew that my life would not be easy growing up, so He placed me in a God-fearing home with my grandparents, so that I could get a solid foundation before having to face my life with my mother. As my grandmother said, I call it my "Ram in the Bush."

I also came to the realization that my mother, with three brain tumors, may not have been able to do any better than she did because, she had a severe disability throughout her life that no one but God knew about. Maybe she couldn't control some of what she did due to those tumors. God helped me to have compassion on her, and I felt bad that she suffered so much and had no help to remedy her situation.

*C*OPING:

After accepting the fact that God placed me in my family for a reason even though I didn't know why, I had to deal with the reality of that fact. Ecclesiastes 4 says, there is "A time to weep, and a time to laugh; A time to mourn, and a time to dance….."

I had to realize that through everything that I went through, without even knowing it, I prayed to God when things got too rough and every time, He got me through every situation. I realized that God was there the whole time, every time. As the songstress Mahalia Jackson says, "My soul looks back and wonders how I got over." I got over with the help of God, my Father. I remembered the times when my mother yelled at me for losing something that belonged to her, like her comb. She would threaten to whip me if I didn't find it. I would pray to God. I would pray God; you are the only one who knows where that comb is. Please help me find it so I won't get a whipping. Please God! Every time He would show me where it was, and I was spared one more time. That prayer I have prayed many times in my life, even now when I lose something, I prayed that prayer and He helped me find it. That helps me even now to cope with what I've been through. God never left me and guided me every step of the way through the power of the Holy Spirit.

Once I understood that my mother was sick her whole life, and despite her disability, I was proud that she was able to excel in her professional life. She excelled so much so that she received recognition from the Mayor of Washington, D.C., for her accomplishments as an excellent government worker. Only God knows why that didn't totally transfer to her personal life, but she was a great employee.

I have learned to cope with the way my life was. TD Jakes once said, "Life is like a coin, you can only spend it once and it can never be spent again. He said the rhythm of life will chase you all the way to the grave; it is fully aligned and fully ordained by God. Time can be erased but never recovered."

Your life may not have been exactly what you would have chosen for you, but God will guide you through every step and ultimately bring you to the place He has ordained and destined for you. Only God knows what it would take to get you there, and He knows your ending from your beginning.

In order to be able to cope with your life as it was, you must trust that God's purpose for you will be fulfilled in the end, because of what He allowed you to go through in your life. All things will work out for our good in the end. It's not always easy to think of things that way, especially when it looks so wrong. My grandmother would always say, "If you haven't been through a certain thing yet, just keep on living." The same is true if you don't understand something, you will eventually understand it, or if you don't, after a while it won't bother you as much.

ACCEPTING:

As I learned to cope with my life, I understood that my life was what it was. I can't go back and change it. If you accept the fact that God had it all in control, then you don't want to go back and change it. You made it through; you got the victory, and that part of your life is over. You can dwell on the bad forever and be miserable, or you can accept what it was and give God the glory for how far he brought you and decide to live the rest of your life in peace. Life is too short and too precious to dwell on the negative. The positive thing about all our lives is that whatever our lot, we can overcome, be content, and live in peace until we die if we want it bad enough. Ecclesiastics 3:2 says there's "A time to be born and a time to die… "A time to kill and a time to heal' A time to break down, and a time to build up…."

We must accept God's plan for our lives because He knows what is best for us. We become better people if we can accept what God has allowed us to go through in order to get us where He wants us to be ultimately. The Bible says, " Trust in God and lean not to your own understanding…" " Our ways are not His ways and our thoughts are not His thoughts…" " Without faith (in God) it is impossible to please God …"

Once we've been through all the "stuff" of our lives, moped about it, gotten angry about it, complained about it, and cried about the mess , then Ecclesiastics 3:6-7 says there's

"A time to gain and a time to lose; A time to keep, and a time to throw away; A time to tear, and A time to sew; a time to keep silence, And a time to speak. I've complained about the bad in my life long enough, and now it's time to move on because I choose too. And God has better for me ahead.

ORGIVING:

Ecclesiastics 3:8 says there's "A time to love, And a time to hate; A time of war, And a time of peace." I realized the most important thing through my sorrows. I realized that in order for me to be healed in the mighty name of Jesus Christ; I had to forgive my parents.

I began my story with feelings of abandonment, feelings of being unloved and neglected. I will end my story with feelings of forgiveness, mercy, and much love. I had to come to a place in my healing process where the only way I could move forward was to forgive my parents. I forgave my father for leaving me and my mother and never being a father to me, nor giving me any financial support. I forgave my mother for the way she treated me when she was depressed or drunk. I thank her for putting a roof over my head, feeding, clothing me, and teaching me what was right and wrong. I thank her for instilling in me the desire to get a good education so I could be financially secure and take care of myself in life. I thank her for showing me love when she could and for causing me to be strong in spirit, opinionated and to fight for what is right. I thank her for showing me how to love others, even when she couldn't always show me that she loved me. It helped me love my husband and children better as a result of feeling unloved.

Most of all I thank my grandparents, especially my grandmother for stepping up to the plate, recognizing my need and accepting the call to meet my needs, and to love me unconditionally.

I thank my husband for never losing faith that I would recover from everything I've been through, for believing in God that He would save our marriage and for waiting and praying for Him to do just that. I thank him for hanging in there with me for better and for worst. God could not have given me a more perfect husband and for that, I am truly grateful!

I thank my children for forgiving me when I was not able to do what I needed to do as their mother and for loving me through it all. I thank my family for not condemning me and for loving me in spite of my short- comings.

More than anything else in this whole world, I wish to thank God for the life He has given me from the beginning. I want to ask Him to forgive me when I doubted if He loved me because He allowed me to go through all the pain. I didn't realize that it was all in order to make me a better child of God and a better human being. I thank God for giving me my parents and my grandparents, my husband, children and my family. I thank Him for allowing me to live the life I've lived as well as helping me to live through it. I thank Him for never leaving me, for leading and guiding me, and for loving me throughout my life and for choosing me from before the beginning of time, to be His child and for loving me enough to lead me into a life with Him forever.

Lord, I thank you for my whole life!

Today, I am delivered from alcohol addiction. I've been sober for almost eleven and a half years. I went back to school and received a bachelors' degree in Grief Counseling/ Bereavement Education. I now give seminars to help those who are hurting from loss. I have mended my relationship with my husband and children and now celebrate the births of two grandsons and expect the birth of a granddaughter in May of 2013.

My faith and walk with the Lord has grown tremendously in the eleven and a half years of my sobriety. I don't need others to validate my importance in this world anymore. I used to want a best friend because that's what my mother said I needed. I have found my best friend in my God and my husband. That's all the friends I need. I've also learned that friends and family can break your heart, too. I have now written my first book and expect to write more in the future. I love the Lord with all my heart, and I'm on my way to heaven when this life on earth is over. Life has been good to me after all and I'm now walking in God's will for my life. It's still not easy at times, and the devil tries to bring up my past to hurt me, sadden, and depress me. "But God" is my fortress and my strength, a very present help in time of trouble, and greater is He that is in me, than he that is in the world. I pray all day every day and take each day one day at a time.

I learned through examining my life as I was recovering from my past that each life is a journey. A journey of ups and downs, tears and laughter, happiness and sorrows, and joys and pain. It was all in God's plan for me. Not that He caused me pain, but that through the pain He allowed for me, it all would work out for my good in the end. God can make sweet, lemonade from sour lemons. He gets the glory in the end, and through the trials and tribulations of our lives, His plan for our life in the end is achieved. What wisdom God has!

I learned that God allows us to go through much of what we go through, so that when he delivers us, we have a testimony, and can plainly state, without reservation, my deliverance is from the Lord and no one else! You realize that without Him in your life (as Marvin Sapp succinctly puts it), I never would have made it. God gets the glory for delivering you from your testimony of pain to the joy of your healing.

I learned that God was with me all of the time ordering my steps and comforting me when the road got too rough. Today, God is still in my life and now that I'm more mature in Him and in life, I can look back over my life and can see Him there, all along the way.

It turns out; I could handle the truth because, "My hope is built on nothing less than Jesus blood and righteousness", and surely, my latter years are greater than my former. God brought me from my testimony to my deliverance. He can bring you from your testimony to your deliverance too if you let Him. I hope you will let Him.

I am moving forward now, and you can as well. Just put your life in His hands and trust in Him! I'm delivered, not from ever hurting again, but from the constant pain of my yesterday. Now my future is bright, and I can truly say, "Deliverance is my testimony now,"

One more thing I would like to say about pain. Growing up with pain, and living in so much pain throughout a whole lifetime I discovered, that while working for 10 years in an elementary school setting, and treating those babies when they came into my health room, I saw the pain in those children's eyes and on their faces. Every time I found out what a particular child was struggling with within their home was probably going to affect the rest of their lives. The pain I saw in those children, was just the beginning, and the pain would mount up over the years and would shape the rest of their lives. I was chosen by God to see the pain in the children's eyes in this season in their lives, and just as he sent me a comforter-He sent them a comforter in me.

God bless you and your future!